The Majestic WONDERS OF AMERICA

Sahale Ridge, North Cascades National Park, Washington. (Bob and Ira Spring Photo)

Home Library Publishing Company
Fort Atkinson, Wisconsin

Palm trees in Everglades National Park, Florida. (Wallace Kirkland Photo)

Contents

Schoodic Peninsula is the only part of the park located on the mainland. (Arthur Griffin Photo)

ACADIA NATIONAL PARK

There is an air of aristocracy about Acadia National Park, but nothing of the lukewarm, weak-tea flavor that sometimes surrounds that word. It is an "aristocrat" in the same sense that the noble Americans who first tried to preserve this place were called by that name — because they could appreciate the many moods of dashing splendor in man and nature.

Maine's Acadia National Park holds itself sometimes aloof in fog-shrouded mystery and sometimes spreads its inner resources of sea and sunshine with a lavish freedom born of ancient riches. Sometimes it flaunts its elegance unconcerned and unquestioning.

It was here, after the Civil War, that the first families of America's inherited wealth came and invited the leisure classes of the world to join them for their summer pleasures. Like called to like, and those of princely tastes came to these islands of royal beauty.

Here is the pink granite of Cadillac Mountain (highest point on the Eastern seaboard); here is the wild crashing sea surging into Thunder Hole; here are the wide, still waters of Somes Sound; here is the variety and grandeur of nature that brought the wealthy socialites of a by-gone age to vacation at Bar Harbor at the turn of this century.

This society has passed away. The Bar Harbor "cottager" whose "cottage" required a dozen household servants to maintain is no longer the chief visitor to Acadia, now, since 1919, a national park (called Lafayette National Park until 1929).

4

Whitecaps rush upon the rocky coast, slowly wearing down the shore line where the struggle between land and the ocean continues. (Grant Heilman Photo)

The new aristocrat, the American vacationer appreciative of nature's wonders, comes bringing his family to this graceful leisure land where the smell of the great spruce forests and the briny tang of the sea, and the tangle of blueberries there for the picking, and the fish-filled streams for his rod and reel, and the lobster traps that are emptied at morning for his purchasing, these all let a man live like a king.

In 1820 Maine became a state and what is now Acadia National Park supported a thinly settled fishing economy.But in the nineteenth century artists rediscovered the beauty of the area, and summer boats from Boston brought it out of the wilderness and within the reach of the affluent, who responded to its loveliness.

In 1901 some of those vacationers, fearful that their island would be ravaged by commercial ex-ploitation, formed a corporation "to acquire and hold for public use lands in Hancock County, Maine, (because of their) beauty (and) historical interest. . . ." In a dozen years they had acquired about six thousand additional acres. The corporation donated this land to the Federal Government, which created out of this gift the fifty square miles that make up Acadia National Park.

East of Mount Desert Island, across Frenchman Bay, there is another portion of the park on Schoodic Peninsula, and southwest of Mount Desert is the park's truly isolated wilderness of Isle au Haut ("High Island").

But to most of the visitors, who arrive in great numbers only to be swallowed by the winding trails and sheltered glens and surf-tossed beaches, Acadia National Park lies along the loop of Ocean Drive , a major park road curving along the Atlantic.

5

CAPE COD
NATIONAL SEASHORE

Cape Cod is a slender rampart jutting more than seventy miles from the Massachusetts coast into the wind and waves of the turbulent Atlantic Ocean. A large section of it became part of the National Park System as a result of the interest and leadership of President John F. Kennedy. The storm-lashed seas surge over the shoals and dash against marine scarps and, miles away, these same seas gently lap the slopes of barrier beaches. The Cape, one of the nation's most dramatic headlands, is the northernmost of our national seashores.

Cape Cod is shaped much like a man flexing his arm muscles. It was named by explorer Bartholomew Gosnold in 1601 for the "grate stoare" of codfish in the vicinity. The Cape, aided by the lengthening of a sandspit called Monomoy Island which extends south from the "elbow" of the Cape, is responsible for the relatively quieter waters of Cape Cod Bay and Nantucket Sound. Sandbars and shoals surrounding the Cape have been a burying ground for ships from the time of the Pilgrims, who first touched New World soil at what is now Provincetown on the extreme northern tip of the Cape.

The exhilarating aspects of winter storms on Cape Cod moved naturalist Henry David Thoreau to write that these periods were the best time to visit the area. Thoreau is credited with giving the name Great Beach to the seaside sands of the Cape. "A man can stand there and put all America behind him," he wrote.

Rooted strongly in sand dunes and silts, the cattails, marsh grass, bearberry, heath and pitch-pine woods stand against the rasping waters, collecting new sand from each windstorm. Glacial movement in the area resulted in an overlapping of northern and southern plant life growing on the Cape. Extensive geological evidence found in the accumulation of glacial drift makes the Cape a lodestone for geo-oceanographers.

Some of the most spectacular sand dune formations are found at Province Lands and Truro at the northern tip. The dunes were formed after

Dead pitch-pine trees are being covered with sand as an active dune moves across the land in the Province lands area. (Gordon Smith Photos)

glacial action thrust clay and boulders into the coastal plains area while the ocean was still shallow. Erosion of the scarps by wave action caused sandbars, then sandspits and later the dunes. As the dunes were formed, they buried whole forests, and when they moved on, remnants of these forests reappeared.

Cape Cod National Seashore, established in 1961, consists of almost 27,000 acres along the outermost one-third of the Cape, primarily facing east and north directly onto the Atlantic.

Opposite: Cape Cod, a long piece of land jutting into the Atlantic from Massachusetts, is a scenic paradise of sand dunes, beach grasses and turbulent ocean breakers.

The most common of the "sea gulls" (left) are the herring gulls and the ring-bellied gulls. (David Dickey Photo) Bodie Island lighthouse (opposite) on the northern end of the Hatteras seashore, stands sentinel against the treacherous sea of North Carolina's Outer Banks. (National Park Service Photo)

CAPE HATTERAS NATIONAL SEASHORE

A northeaster storm on Cape Hatteras in North Carolina has to be experienced to be believed. Raging wind blows sand with such force that it can be heard hitting a building, and the brushy plants bend away from the gusts, as if bowing to this master of violent nature. The seas crash their breakers into the shore, spray is hurled into the wind, and skies are ominously dark, the air filled with a cold, misty rain. A walk along the beach at this time is a walk in total loneliness, an experience unique to a place facing the sea.

Hours later, after the storm has passed, the beach takes on a different character. A warm breeze ruffles the drying sea oats and the setting sun plays with the clouds. A ghost crab scurries into the wet sand at your approach; scavenging shorebirds look for culinary delights at the edge of each dying breaker.

Cape Hatteras National Seashore was established in 1953. It covers forty-five square miles stretched along seventy miles of shores of three barrier islands, each separated by an inlet. The eight villages are excluded from the seashore.

Visitor centers are located at the Hatteras and Bodie Island lighthouses and at Ocracoke village. Seven campgrounds are within the seashore's boundaries. The entire beach length is open for swimming.

At the tip of Cape Hatteras is the tallest lighthouse in the United States, 192 feet above low-tide level. Built in 1870, it is one of three on the Cape and easily recognized by "barberpole" striping.

Ocracoke, Hatteras and Bodie islands are barrier islands believed to have been formed by ocean currents and wave action on what were originally shoals to the east of the present shoreline. The islands are not more than three miles in width and are covered with sand dunes which have not been stabilized and are still moving.

The head of the Cape, about three miles south of the Hatteras Lighthouse, provides a close-up view of the dangerous Diamond Shoals. The sudden shallow water a couple of hundred feet out from the beach combined with the mixing of the two large ocean currents causes waves to tumble over each other at angles, making a thunderous roar and much foam.

NIAGARA FRONTIER STATE PARKS

The Niagara River, actually a strait, flows in a northerly direction for only thirty-four miles connecting Lake Erie to Lake Ontario. Erie, however, is 572 feet above sea level, and Ontario, 246 feet. Niagara Falls is the result of this great drop of 326 feet along the river's course, most of it occurring in a collected series of falls and rapids that has the high falls as the central attraction. Here, at the ''Thundering Waters,'' as the Indians named the spot, fifteen million cubic feet of water a minute plunge down the escarpment. Nearly a mile wide at this point, the falls are divided into two main areas, the American and Canadian or Horseshoe Falls.

The Canadian Falls carries ninety-four percent of the water and has a crest line of 3,010 feet and a drop of 158 feet. The American Falls has a crest line of 1,060 feet, but a drop of 167 feet. While the foot of the American Falls is shallow and rocky, the pool below the Canadian Falls reaches a depth of 160 feet.

Between them is Bridal Veil Falls, well known as the sight favored by honeymooners. Dramatic views can be seen from Luna Island that is connected by a foot bridge to Goat Island, which in turn is connected to the bank by the American Rapids Bridge.

The area around the falls was strategically important in colonial times, since it is the only break in an all-water route between the upper St. Lawrence River and the upper Great Lakes. Niagara has become a world-renowned hydroelectric center and the nucleus of a well-known manufacturing community.

The State Reservation at Niagara was established in 1885 and is called the first state park in New York. A dozen state parks have since been established in the area, sufficient to accommodate and offer recreational opportunities for the many visitors who come to see the falls, this legend of living water.

The tremendous falls along the Niagara River
include the American at the left, Bridal Veil in the center,
and the Canadian or Horseshoe on the right.
(H. Armstrong Roberts Photo)

Serene Spruce Knob Lake in the Monongahela forest is set amid the ancient Allegheny Mountains. (National Forest Service Photos)

MONONGAHELA NATIONAL FOREST

Man cannot cast his shadow on the rising of the sun, or halt the flow of the winds, or alter the rhythm of the waves. But he can enrich his humanity with appreciation of the greater world that lies above and beyond his own.

Wilderness is the tangible essence of the greater world placed within our grasp to touch and feel, and to test our sensitivity.

In Monongahela National Forest, almost a million acres in eastern West Virginia, man can come close and touch the wilderness.

Spruce Knob, the highest point in West Virginia (4,860 feet), is bordered by many species of plant life found far south of their normal range. Roadside overlooks are numerous at high elevations, with beautiful vistas into valleys of both Virginia and West Virginia. A trail leads to the cool summit.

A unique natural area where orchids and cranberries grow in mountain bogs — similar to vegetation in the low areas of Maine — is the subject of the Cranberry Mountain Visitor Center near Richwood. Two miles west of the center a self-guiding boardwalk trail leads across a small portion of the famous Cranberry Glades and introduces the visitor to plants, birds and mammals of the northern tundra. The soil is mainly sphagnum and sedge peat up to eleven feet deep underlain with algal ooze and clay. Carnivorous sundew and horned bladderwort, rare in the southern Alleghenies, are highly esteemed.

In Spruce Knob-Seneca Rocks National Recreation Area, whitewater canoeing is popular with experts on swiftflowing streams that form the headwaters of the Potomac River. An especially favorite course starts at Mouth of Seneca and winds downstream through canyons for fifteen miles. In addition, Seneca Rocks at Mouth of Seneca is one of the highest, most impressive rock formations in the East. Rock climbers come from hundreds of miles away to test their skills.

One hundred million people live within five hundred miles of the parallel mountain ridges contained within the national recreation area. But its purpose is not only to provide recreation for today but to "preserve important resources for future generations." Accordingly, the quiet green character in the heart of the hills is protected through cooperative regional planning to "promote a harmonious and unified development of the national recreation area and the surrounding region." This beautiful but economically depressed region may yet come into its own through the wise use of its rich recreational resources.

12

The unforgettable sound of the elk rises to a bugle tone heard for miles, then flattens out to a grunt and bay.

MAMMOTH CAVE NATIONAL PARK

The darkness grips the visitor, then the depths slowly come into focus as the eyes adjust themselves to the underworld of Kentucky's Mammoth Cave, which has been a lure to awe-struck men since it was first trod by primitives.

It is still a place of mystery, this partially unexplored hollow land beneath the surface. The ancients braved superstition and penetrated more than three miles of its vaulted passages, seeking gypsum. The dry, even temperatured air has preserved for centuries their worn-out sandals and burnt torch ends, scattered here and there among footprints before sheer walls hacked with rude stone tools. Why they sought the soft mineral is not known. The remains of one of them is still there, his body mummified after he was crushed by a six-ton boulder while gathering the stone 2,400 years ago.

The yawning cavern was rediscovered by an unknown white man in 1798, and a few years later by another seeking saltpeter, or potassium nitrate, a prime ingredient of black gunpowder.

The bored-out tree trunks used to carry the chemical solution to vats are still here, along with other well-preserved artifacts of the operation.

The saltpeter industry died after the War of 1812; then began Mammoth Cave's career as a tourist attraction, although much of it remained unexplored. Jenny Lind sang here, her voice echoing and reechoing through the rooms of stone. Edwin Booth, the great Shakespearian actor, intoned the philosophy of Hamlet in this apt surrounding.

In 1837 a fifteen-year-old boy named Stephen Bishop, among the cave's first guides, crossed the Bottomless Pit on a slender pole, opening the way to extensive uncharted corridors and passages. Bishop guided the many eminent scientists who visited the cave thereafter, and achieved world renown before he died in 1859. He is buried in what is now the park. Later the cave became an underground tuberculosis sanitarium. It was proposed as a national park in 1911; that was accomplished thirty years later.

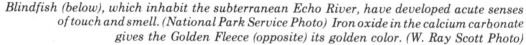

Blindfish (below), which inhabit the subterranean Echo River, have developed acute senses of touch and smell. (National Park Service Photo) Iron oxide in the calcium carbonate gives the Golden Fleece (opposite) its golden color. (W. Ray Scott Photo)

SHENANDOAH NATIONAL PARK
and BLUE RIDGE PARKWAY

This is a humble place where beauty is quiet and does not shout, where there is a tranquility, a charm of blushing shyness that only gradually captures the visitor's awareness. But once its cup of gentle refreshment is drunk, one will find his pleasure.

This is Shenandoah, cradled against the breast of gentle mountains grown mellow with the age of the eastern half of our continent, spread in a generous north-south sweep down northwestern Virginia, encompassing great but not unconquerable mountains and brooks running in a grandfatherly way through stately trees.

Yet, compared with other national parks, Shenandoah seems a lesser light until first the geological history is realized; finally its subtlety shines and one realizes there are few places left that can match its serenity. "Oh, Shenandoah, I Love Your Daughter," pleads the American folk song, and one wonders if its composer refers to the daughter of an Indian chief or the land named for the sachem. It is moot, for Shenandoah whispers of love, love of the land and its creatures.

These scene of green coolness and a long mountain range like a vein of blue is a great gift, for within a day's drive, over half of the nation's population can escape the tedium and anxieties of urban existence and sink into its quiet pleasure.

The Blue Ridge Mountains were first seen by Captain John Smith, and later by Alexander Spotswood, the colonial governor of Virginia who crossed near what is now Swift Run Gap. George Freeman Pollock visited the Blue Ridge in 1886, and inspired by its beauty, spent a lifetime building a resort on Stony Man Mountain to let others succumb to the region's charm.

Pollock and friends proposed Shenandoah to a national committee, formed in 1925 to seek suitable park sites in the East. It was not an easy time for them; they struggled most of a night answering the committee's questionnaire, finishing it only a scant few hours ahead of the deadline.

Harry Flood Byrd, Sr., then governor of Virginia, supported their proposal and appointed his commissioner of conservation and development to oversee the purchase of lands for Shenandoah. The state legislature appropriated a million dollars, a vast sum in the time of hard cash, to help the park along. Added to it was $1.25 million in the pennies, nickels and dimes of Virginians and others.

It was not until the eve of the Fourth of July, 1936, that Shenandoah National Park was a reality. President Franklin Delano Roosevelt dedicated it in ceremonies at Big Meadows, for the "recreation and re-creation which we shall find here."

Re-creation. It is two things spelled one way; only the pronunciation is different. For many who see Shenandoah, the accent is on the first syllable, for they are *re*-created here. They usually come by the Skyline Drive, a winding, 105-mile road threading across the crest of the Blue Ridge, offering seventy-five parking overlooks of the valleys and mountain slopes. Often they stop to leave the pavement and walk some of the two hundred miles of foot trails.

Walking is the best way to enjoy the subtle pleasures of the park, such as seeing water shift its course to the other side of a rock, or feeling beneath one's feet the crunch of the brown, needle-strewn floor of the forest. A few yards beyond may be a handful of gnarled apple trees, unpruned for generations, surrounding a small clearing being rapidly overgrown with trees.

This is an old part of our land, more than a billion years in creation. Craggy peaks were smoothed by time into the gentle slopes of today, often wearing a mantle of the blue haze which gave the famous Blue Ridge its name.

The Blue Ridge Parkway, separately administered but actually an extension of Shenandoah and Great Smoky national parks, winds slowly from its lowest elevation crossing the James River in Virginia upward to its highest point of more than six thousand feet in elevation in the Balsams south of Asheville, North Carolina. From it one can see the rolling hills of the Virginia Piedmont, across the fertile fields of the Great Valley, to the Alleghenies and then onward to the Black Mountains and the Great Smokies. Adjacent to the parkway are three national forests.

The frequent bluish haze seen about the rolling hills of the Virginia Piedmont, for which Blue Ridge Parkway was named, is evident at Craggy Gardens near Asheville, North Carolina. (David Muench Photo)

The Little Pigeon River (opposite) adds to gentle scenic beauty at Smoky. A sunset at Mount Le Conte (right) colors the skies with a prism of hues. (National Park Service Photos)

GREAT SMOKY MOUNTAINS NATIONAL PARK

Rising high between the states of North Carolina and Tennessee are the Great Smoky Mountains, the highest range of the Appalachian Chain which extends from Gaspé, Canada, to northern Georgia. The lofty range of the Smokies is the climax of the Appalachians and is the backbone of Great Smoky Mountains National Park.

Known as the cradle of eastern American vegetation, this area supplied plants and animals to the land exposed for the first time in thousands of years as the glacial ice sheet retreated northward. Primeval and timeworn as they are, vegetation densely covers the Smokies with a sea of green from base to summits, some rising more than six thousand feet.

At first, the Great Smokies may appear to have a certain sameness, then suddenly the delight unfolds: The presence of junglelike plant life together with the prevalent haze charms many who visit the park. Wisps of fog rise from the valley as low-hanging clouds roll through the gaps following the summer rainstorms when most of the precipitation falls. Blue, cold water falls into rushing streams, tipping over the edges of stone after stone. A half-light hovers at the doorway to a mysterious, beckoning cave.

The mountains are steep, but not nearly unconquerable, faced with high rock, but not having the sheer face of the Tetons. Nature has mellowed the Great Smokies with time, gently filling deep valleys and rounding sharp peaks so that they have a graceful, undulating rhythm.

The trees are a part of an ecological cycle existing because of the protection given the region by its national park status. Their life is interrelated with smaller plants, the rhododendron, ferns and a gamut of wildflowers. They, in turn, are links in the chain of survival for fifty species of mammals, two hundred types of birds, and fish hovering silently in deep stream-pools.

This country attracted settlers who were hardy, self-sufficient people mostly from Scotland and England. They vied for hunting and fishing lands with the Cherokee Indians whose reservation is now adjacent to the park on the south. The customs, speech and names of those pioneers cling to the region today.

Some of their descendants lived in Cades Cove, Tennessee, which was an isolated community until World War I and some of its citizens joined the armed services. It was seven years after the armistice before a good road linked this tiny town with the world around it.

Today, there are nearly eight hundred square miles for the people's pleasure in this region where all that is gentle and soft is supreme; a mass of green winter and summer, a climate kind to man, an abundant supply of water to nourish the natural treasures preserved in these venerable mountains.

19

Okefenokee Swamp is characterized by dark waters and strings of Spanish moss festooning the trees. One of the largest swamps in the nation, most of it is protected as a wildlife refuge. (National Park Service Photo)

OKEFENOKEE NATIONAL WILDLIFE REFUGE

Those who want to study an unimpaired swampland environment should come to Okefenokee. One of the largest, oldest and most primitive protected swamps in the United States, it covers 412,000 acres in extreme southeastern Georgia. Vegetation includes many huge cypress trees mixed with blackgum and redbay. The uplands around the swamp and the islands within it are covered principally with pine and occasional hardwood patches, called hammocks. From May to October the evergreen foliage of the gordonia, one of the swamp's most distinctive trees, is spotted with large white flowers.

About sixty thousand acres of Okefenokee is prairie, or open marsh. During spring these areas are carpeted with white and yellow water lilies, yellow-spiked "neverwet," white floating hearts, purple bladderwort and pickerelweed.

Sometimes a large piece of peat will break away from the swamp bottom and float on the surface. Smaller plants take root until trees and large brush grow on these floating islands. Locally called "houses" because of the many animals and birds that live and nest on them, the islets frequently become anchored by the trees extending their roots down through the water to the bed of peat below, which may be as thick as twenty feet. The stamping of feet on one of these peat islands will cause the nearby trees to shake, thus the Choctaw name *owaquaphenogau* ("Land of the Trembling Earth"). Okefenokee is simply an anglicized version of this Indian word.

A major characteristic of Okefenokee is the Spanish moss, which is actually an air-breathing plant. Found throughout the Southern states, it festoons all the swamp vegetation with long, flowing draperies of brown and gray.

A few small inlets at the north end of the swamp furnish the only source of water streaming into Okefenokee. The water, coffee-colored due to tannic acids from partially submerged trees, moves slowly through the swamp to the two outlets at the south — the Suwanee River (immortalized in song by Stephen Foster) which drains into the Gulf of Mexico, and St. Mary's River which flows past Jacksonville into the Atlantic.

The most readily recognizable animal in the swamp is the American alligator, rare in almost every other part of the country, but abundant here. This holdover from prehistoric times is known throughout the United States, even by small school children ("A is for Alligator"), as a vicious villain; while actually, unlike its cousin the crocodile, it will normally avoid man unless

A common egret rests in a slash-pine tree. This bird has up to fifty long plumes on its back during breeding season. (Michael Dunn Photo)

provoked. Until recent laws made their illegal trade unprofitable, poachers sold their hides to handbag and shoe manufacturerers, and reduced their numbers until they were becoming an endangered species.

Other animals in the swamp include opossums, otters, raccoons, white-tailed deer, black bears and wild turkeys. The Eastern spadefoot toad, with smooth instead of warty skin, rings out its call on spring nights, and the cottonmouth water moccasin, shy but with a deadly poisonous bite, slithers through the waters in search of frogs.

Practically all of the Atlantic Flyway's species of ducks are here in season, and many stay all year. The anhinga, or snakebird, a large black bird that feeds solely on fish, rests frequently on branches with outstretched wings drying in the sun. Its name comes from its ability to swim completely submerged except for its long snakelike neck. Sandhill cranes majestically fly up from the water, long necks extended, and egrets and herons stalk through the swamp waters in search of food. During the day a red-shouldered hawk may scream overhead, and at night barred owls hoot in the darkness, sending echoes among the cypresses.

Four-fifths of the swamp is under the protection of the Bureau of Sport Fisheries and Wildlife as the Okefenokee National Wildlife Refuge. The establishment of this refuge in 1937 marked the culmination of a long fight to save the swamp from "developers." Beginning in the sixteenth century, when Hernando de Soto may have explored the swamp, Okefenokee was threatened with drainage and timber cutting.

Stephen Foster State Park, in the interior of the refuge, can be reached via a paved road through the southwestern portion, and a number of facilities, including cottages and a picnic area, are available here.

Early-day naturalist William Bartram wrote in 1791 of a belief held by the Creek Indians that an island existed in the middle of the great swamp which was the most blissful place on earth. It was inhabited by a tribe whose women were "incomparably beautiful" while the men were fierce and cruel. After gliding silently along on dark waters beneath eerily draped cypresses and seeing alligators peer up from the water surface with inquisitive eyes, a visitor may wonder about this old legend. Certainly there are many unexpected and fascinating pleasures to be seen in this incomparable swampland environment.

Dead logs lay across a vast swamp which is interlaced with placid waterways. (Wallace Kirkland Photo)

EVERGLADES NATIONAL PARK

Quiet, calm, flat, mysterious — the Everglades are a unique part of the American landscape, the largest subtropical wilderness in North America.

Lake Okeechobee, massively spilling over to the north, created this river of grass, broad, short and shallow, with multifarious water creatures — wading birds, alligators, turtles, otter and fish — thriving in and about its swampy lushness in Florida.

All this lush, growing green can be seen best from the jungle spots on elevated islands called hammocks. Towering trees, dangling vines, carpets of ferns, West Indian in character, flourish here, where thrive the Liguus trees snails, so beautiful in aspect and so rarely seen elsewhere.

Here, where dark, tangled coastal forests drove Spanish horsemen to more maneuverable coasts, are ghostly clusters of mangrove trees, cypress heads, bayheads and stands of Caribbean pine. Many trees grow above tangles of crooked, interlocking roots which sustain their trunks above the water. The pines are slender-tufted, fire-resistant and fire-perpetuated and they have been used extensively in the building of termite and rot-resistant structures.

The Everglades thermometers do not fluctuate sharply during the two characteristic seasons, the wet summer and dry winter. During the rainy season, great cloud formations are sculptured battlements over the terrain, colored and dominated by dark thunderheads. Sometimes a hurricane will move in from the tropical seas, wreaking havoc: Sea beasts are washed ashore, vegetation stands bare and windstripped, water everywhere, salt and fresh, inundates the land.

Once a rustic fishing village, Flamingo is now a gateway to the water wilderness of the park, the bays and rivers. Along the rich and intriguing Florida Bay shore there is no perceptible dividing line between land and sea. Beyond is Cape Sable, a pristine retreat whose immaculately white sands shelter the eggs of huge, lumbering loggerhead turtles, which may grow to weigh half a ton.

Midway to Flamingo from park headquarters, the salt area begins. This enormous brackish zone is nature's inaccessible nursery for numerous game fish and the coveted pink shrimp. Spawn and prawn, a swampy matrix of infant, edible fish life, is permitted to grow and eventually fills the demands of commercial and sport fish operations amid the Keys and along the Gulf Coast.

Here, too, are the mangrove trees, grotesque on the aforesaid prop roots. The citizen of Copenhagen would wonder at the rookeries of storks in this region, increasing and multiplying, a continent removed from the storied stork-nest roofs of Denmark.

The dark memory of the ruthless plume hunters can be vividly recalled in this expanse, where exploiters once threatened to bring exquisite species of waterfowl to extinction.

The park by night is a jungle of sound and movement. The cries of night birds, the watery thrashings of alligators seeking garfish in the sloughs, the crackling predatory movements of raccoons and panthers, the choruses of insects, toads and frogs arise in sporadic crescendo, and all are weirdly, momentarily illuminated by streaks of lightning in the ebony sky.

The experienced explorer knows the threat and rudeness of the terrain — a few poisonous snakes (including the diamondback rattlesnake), trees which shake off blister-yielding rain drippings, the pits and pinnacles of the trails. Add to this the steamy humidity of summer, the severe winds and drenching rains. But the prize is worth the worry and strain. It now is attainable in areas of minimal discomfort for the bird-watcher, the naturalist, the boater. The strange beauty of the Everglades is ours.

Shady stretches of beach provide encompassing views of the Gulf of Mexico. (National Park Service Photos)

GULF ISLANDS NATIONAL SEASHORE

Wide, gently sloping beaches of unusually fine, white "sugar" sand, clear blue waters reminiscent of Caribbean bays, unique flora and fauna, and several historically important forts are the characteristics of Gulf Islands National Seashore. Consisting of about 13,600 acres of barrier and offshore islands stretching 150 miles from Florida to Mississippi, the seashore is a prime example of what dedicated citizens can do for the preservation of our natural resources.

Citizen interest in these islands was developed in the 1960's when it was learned that sea erosion was undermining Fort Massachusetts on Mississippi's Ship Island, now included within the seashore. They appealed to their Congressmen and Senators for Federal help in preserving the fort, which was further damaged in September 1965 by Hurricane Betsy. Erosion would not wait for legislation, however, and local residents formed an organization called Save the Fort, Inc., which gained widespread publicity and enough contributions to erect a protective wall around the old structure. A bill authorizing the proposed seashore passed Congress and was signed by President Richard M. Nixon in January 1971.

Saved from further commercial development are some of Mississippi's offshore islands, namely Horn, Petit Bois (meaning "little woods" and locally pronounced "petty boy") and Ship Islands, and in Florida, parts of Santa Rosa Island

Beach morning glories spread their creamy white-yellow flowers.

(formerly the Santa Rosa National Monument which was deactivated by the Secretary of the Interior in 1946), the eastern half of Perdido Key across the channel from Santa Rosa, and sections of Naval Life Oaks Reservation and the Pensacola Naval Air Station, both on the mainland. The two state areas are separated by Alabama's Gulf Coast.

Santa Rosa, a long, thin barrier island, is significant because of its sandy beaches and clear waters. On the western tip of the island lies Fort Pickens, an old brick fort built in 1834 to protect the important deepwater harbor at Pensacola. Before that, the site had been occupied by Spanish, French and British.

Flora in the seashore is extremely varied. For example, Horn Island contains over 204 species of plants. Slim slash-pine trees fight to survive the salt and sand driven by stormy winds. Some of the sand dunes have been stabilized by species of magnolia, palmetto and live oak, while the unstabilized dunes are mostly covered with beach grass and sea oats. The 1,300-acre Naval Live Oaks Reservation is a beautiful stand of large live oaks and represents the nation's first attempt at conservation: President John Quincy Adams set aside the area in 1828 to save these rare oaks from being used for shipbuilding.

Fur-bearing animals find little on which to survive, and rabbits and opossums are the only two mammals still fairly common on the islands. The monument provides many places for the Gulf's increasingly rare sea turtles to lay their eggs, and it is the only habitat for a species of beach mouse which has developed a very light coloration to blend into the white sand.

A great number of birds nest within the seashore, especially on Horn and Petit Bois islands. Here the interior ponds, lagoons and marshes serve as wintering grounds for blue and snow geese and several species of ducks. The beaches support laughing gulls and Sandwich and royal terns; redhead ducks are abundant on the shallow Gulf waters. Other birds include common and snowy egrets; green, great blue and Louisiana herons; willets; snowy and Wilson's plovers; sanderlings; American oystercatchers; killdeer; and occasional ospreys and frigate birds.

Isle Royale has many moods. In one of the most charming, a tranquil beauty descends with night upon the numerous lakes and islands of the archipelago, where man can find the isolated splendor that comes with being in the north woods. (National Park Service Photo)

ISLE ROYALE NATIONAL PARK

Isle Royale, now north woods wilderness held in a lake's solitude, is visibly haunted by the grace and majesty of its geological past. This handsomely endowed protectorate of vast Lake Superior, in Michigan, and twenty-two miles from the Minnesota shore, is enveloped by the greatest of the Great Lakes, the lake which marks the site of the southern end of an ancient and possibly one of the highest mountain ranges that ever existed on our continent.

The formation of Lake Superior and perhaps Isle Royale itself is explained eloquently by Rutherford Platt in *The Great American Forest*: "Through timeless eras . . . in many places the uplift of mountains so weakened the edge of the Canadian Shield (a shield is a broad, massive, symmetrical rock upheaval) that it gave way, . . . creating depressions for future lakes and river valleys."

The pure copper deposits of Isle Royale and even the mineral riches of its geologic cousin the Mesabi Range are explained by Platt: "The Canadian Shield became the pedestal of the North Woods." He describes the intrusions of plutonic minerals and ravaging of the area's surface by glaciers, the outcroppings of rock in which, on Isle Royale itself, the Indians found copper "so pure it can be used without smelting. This was the source of copper for Indian artifacts found scattered far and wide through the American wilderness."

Isle Royale, forty-five miles in length, is redolent with the ancient history of Indian copper miners, who reportedly worked there four thousand years ago. Its fjord-like harbors, sheltered bays and interior, parallel ridges attaining a height of seven hundred feet, were first looked upon by white men in 1699. These were French explorers who named the island for Louis XIV.

The canoe yielded to the motor launch, the small boat to the excursion vessel. Hotels and summer homes were beginning to multiply. A cry was raised and the administration of the second great conservationist Roosevelt responded to their reasoned pleas. In 1936, Franklin Delano Roosevelt signed the Isle Royale National Park Act resulting in its establishment four years later.

27

A wave crashes into Chapel Rock, clearly demonstrating how Lake Superior's waters were able to carve these magnificent Pictured Rocks. (National Park Service Photo)

PICTURED ROCKS NATIONAL LAKESHORE

From the waters of Lake Superior, the largest freshwater lake in the world, the afternoon sun brings out the deep colors of the rocky cliffs — the reds, greens, browns and purples — and the various shapes of the rocks are accentuated by long shadows. Inland the sun sparkles on the lakes and cascading streams, and the maples and birches ruffle in the breeze. The scent of pine drifts down the hillsides and, far away, a coyote howls. It is not hard to imagine a young Indian brave named Hiawatha paddling his birch-bark canoe on these lake waters. For this is the land of the Gitche-Gumee, the shining Big-Sea-Water, and nearby is the wigwam of Nokomis, who raised Hiawatha. It was at his wedding feast that Pau-Puk-Keemis danced on the beach and kicked up the sands that are called the Grand Sable Dunes.

Although Longfellow's epic poem is fiction, much of his setting was based upon the Pictured Rocks area of Michigan's Upper Peninsula. The Chippewa Indians resided here for many years, and French explorers and missionaries, including Pierre Radisson and Father Marquette, knew the area well.

The main single attraction are the Pictured Rocks themselves, fifteen miles of multicolored sandstone cliffs rising abruptly from the lake as much as two hundred feet. In the never-ending struggle against erosion, these rocks are fighting a losing battle, for the waves, rain and frost have carved arches, columns, promontories and thunder caves out of the cliffs. Groundwater, seeping to various sandstone levels and collecting minerals and chemicals on the way, drips down the sides of the eroded sculptures, depositing the staining chemicals. The names describe the formations: Miners Castle, Chapel Rock, Lovers Leap, Rainbow Cave and the Battleships. In the early 1900's Grand Portal, a magnificent series of several honeycombed arches jutting six hundred feet into the lake, collapsed, leaving lesser arches, amphitheaters and debris.

Pictured Rocks National Lakeshore, approved by Congress in 1966, protects thirty-five miles of Lake Superior shoreline from Grand Marais to Munising. It also includes many thousands of acres of forested slopes and inland waters.

A birch tree frames the summer greenery surrounding a beaver pond in Voyageurs. (Les Blacklock Photo)

VOYAGEURS NATIONAL PARK

During the eighteenth and early nineteenth centuries when ladies of European society demanded the best North American fur for their clothing, those waters in northern Minnesota rang with the singing of French-Canadian *voyageurs*. These rugged adventurers paddled and portaged in their fragile, birchbark canoes thousands of tons of furs and trade goods yearly over the three-thousand-mile waterway extending from Montreal to Fort Chipewyan on Lake Athabaska in what is now upper Alberta.

The movement to create a Voyageurs National Park began in 1891 when the State of Minnesota requested congressional authorization for a

Dark evergreens stand out against autumn's light-colored deciduous trees along developed Ash River (above), just outside the southern boundary of the park, which can be seen in the distance. A birch tree (opposite) is gracefully silhouetted against the Minnesota sky. (National Park Service Photos)

national park in the Ontario-Minnesota border wilderness. After many years of controversy, the park service finally recommended the region east of International Falls around the Kabetogama Peninsula, and in January 1971 President Richard M. Nixon signed a bill authorizing the nation's thirty-sixth national park, just west of the Boundary Waters Canoe Area.

Consisting of 139,000 acres of north woods country plus eighty thousand acres of water, the park includes large Kabetogama Lake and parts of Rainy and Namekan lakes.

Four times ice sheets edged down from the north, grinding the land bare, and each time these spectacular forests grew back. During this last century, many thousands of acres of virgin pine forests in this region were stripped clean by loggers, but the land is now covered once again with large second-growth pines, firs, spruce, aspens and birches.

All of these natural features provide food and shelter for a wide variety of wildlife.White-tailed deer and black bears are common, as are smaller animals such as minks, otters, bobcats and rabbits and beavers. The park service plans to reintroduce caribou and increase the moose population. Hawks, golden eagles and a wide variety of songbirds and waterfowl make Voyageurs their home during season. The lake sturgeon, a rare and endangered fish,lives in some larger lakes.

One writer has said of the *voyageur*, "His canoe has long since vanished from the northern waters, his red cap is seen no more, a bright spot against the blue of Lake Superior; ..." But his land remains, the sky-blue water and north woods forests that he knew, preserved in this park for future generations.

BADLANDS NATIONAL MONUMENT

The erosion-scarred landscape of Badlands National Monument has the eerie look of a city that was designed, and later deserted, by a mad architect. The land between the Cheyenne and White rivers in southwestern South Dakota is austere and harsh. Sheer cliffs and jagged peaks form skylines of fantastic shapes.

The Dakota Indians and neighboring tribes called this barren land *mako sica,* meaning, "land bad," because it was an area of hardship for travelers. Early French-Canadian trappers appropriately termed it *les mauvaises terres a traverser,* "bad lands to travel across." Settlers later called it simply the Badlands, a name applied later to similar eroded areas in many sections of the country.

Bison, bear, elk, white-tailed and mule deer, pronghorns, Audubon bighorn sheep, gray wolves and beaver were originally native to the area and once plentiful. But the invasion of settlers, hunters and trappers in the late nineteenth century caused a serious reduction of wildlife populations. In 1919 a game investigator reported that inquiries at farms and ranches of the area revealed the fact that not even a coyote had been seen in the Badlands for more than a year.

In an effort to help restore wildlife patterns, the National Park Service reintroduced bighorn and bison into the monument in the early 1960's. Rocky Mountain bighorn sheep were settled there, but difficulties were such that five years later the flock numbered only ten. Bison, on the other hand, adapted readily to their old haunts after being brought back in 1963.

The Badlands, declared a monument in 1939, is a harsh and inhospitable environment for all plants because moisture is scarce and rainfall sometimes runs off without soaking into the ground. High temperatures in summer and relatively cold temperatures in winter also limit plant life.

Nonetheless, some three hundred kinds of plants grow there. Although cliffsides and peaks are barren because erosion tears out most plants attempting to root, about half of the monument surfaces are covered with carpets of cactus and other growth.

Constant flux is the only certainty in the Badlands of South Dakota
where erosion repatterns the land each generation. (National Park Service Photo)

MARK TWAIN NATIONAL FOREST

Missouri was formerly almost completely covered by magnificent stands of hardwoods. Intensive logging depleted the tree supply to less than a third of what it was. Two national forests nurture much of what remains — the Clark and the Mark Twain in the southern part of the state, along the edge of the Ozark Plateau. The second-growth forests of hardwoods spreads throughout the half million acres of the Mark Twain forest.

Rivers are the living arteries of most forests, and in the Ozarks, there are about twenty streams spring-born and spring-fed. Some have been dammed to form lakes of tremendous size — arenas for motor-boating, water skiing, bass fishing and resort camping. To some, however, true Ozarkiana is still to be found in a float down a clear, swift-running stream like the Eleven Point, which bends and winds between steep hollows and towering bluffs of the Mark Twain forest.

The Eleven Point is a favorite in southern Missouri for float fishing and camping. Such travel is in the Ozark tradition, recalling the days when each farm had a landing with a skiff or two (known as a flatboat, Long John, or just plain johnboat) tied to a handy tree root and when it was easier to get around on the back streams than on the back roads.

The Eleven Point River meanders without hurry or concern through the picturesque Ozark hills east of Thomasville, its course cut in the shadows of steep bluffs, through forested sloping valleys and low-lying pasturelands.

Greer Spring in the Mark Twain forest helps to make the Eleven Point River a remarkably clear stream. (National Forest Service Photo)

The great rock called Devils Tower has been an object for legends and stunts. (National Park Service Photo)

DEVILS TOWER NATIONAL MONUMENT

A mighty laccolith resembling a petrified tree stump thrusts itself eight hundred feet skyward from a rounded hill above the Belle Fourche River Valley in northeast Wyoming. The massive gray and buff stone — a dramatic landmark northwest of Sundance, Wyoming — has a startling appearance from all sides.

A geological prodigy, this rock upthrust had a place in Indian legends of the region. The Kiowa Indians called the place *mato teepe*, meaning "bear's lodge." The Cheyenne legend termed it "bad god's tower." Explorers used it as a guide point, and this landmark came under intense scientific interest at the end of the nineteenth century. It was set aside as Devils Tower National Monument in 1906, the first U.S. national monument to be authorized by a president under the Antiquities Act of 1906.

Volcanic activity, deep inside the earth, caused an explosive upsurge of magma here about fifty million years ago. Devils Tower was created when the volcanic thrust pushed this particular mass of molten materials only to the surface — or perhaps somewhat below the surface — where it cooled. Erosion in the intervening millions of years, possibly during some ancient deluge, gradually eroded away softer formations of surrounding earth and rock.

Devils Tower is more than a thousand feet in diameter at its base. Its top, measuring 200 by 400 feet, is 1,280 feet above the Belle Fourche River and 5,117 feet above sea level. It is the tallest rock formation of its kind in the United States, and geologists continue to study its strange origin and peculiarities.

Because it is comprised of crystallized molten rock and some sedimentary forms, the composition of the towering rock has a strikingly multicolored appearance as seen from various vantage points in its forest-green and grassy setting. Looking from near the base, the giant pillar has a curiously fluted look, appearing as though the middle part of the tower is made of columns bound by well-developed, open joints. These open, smooth joints, however, seem to join in a weld as they taper together at the higher points.

The legends of the Indians indicate that the rock was a fascination for the first Americans. The Kiowa story detailed how several flower-gathering Indian maidens, being pursued by an angry bear, jumped onto this rock (then normal sized) which was quickly elevated to its present height by their powerful god. The Cheyenne legend, in which young braves were principals, was somewhat similar in that it also involved huge bears. Attempting to scale the heights, the bears were supposed to have left claw marks — the flutings — along the tower sides.

GRAND TETON NATIONAL PARK

Vast, snow-covered graph lines of gray are etched upon the spring-breath blue of sky, mirroring their mighty heights upon apparently miniscule lakes below; giant shadows are cast across already-dark forests of deep green.

The Tetons of Wyoming give no hint of their ascension, no foothills lead the viewer's eye to this grandiose essence of all the beauty that the mountains of the West have to offer; for here there is a glassy lake, a stand of conifers and suddenly there are those incredible peaks.

Through the great valley pours the Snake River, a wide and rushing stream flowing clearly across a deep bed of sand and stones where game-fish dart in cool depths and to which adventurous man escapes for a few moments to ply the current in a fragile rubber raft.

Lakes lie among the green like a cool morning's dew on a field of newly mown grain, glistening in the sun between the natural fist of the Tetons on one side and wind-whispered forests of conifers on the other. Here and there are sun-splashed meadows, a crown of green wearing the royal jewels of complacent wildflowers and streams trickling thorugh rich, black humus where the colors of spring blooms push their way through the floor of last autumn's fallen leaves. This forest is not silent, for there is the pleasure grunt of the moose with newfound food, the chattering of thousands of birds feeding and the scrape then crash of a long-dead tree as the black bear uncovers a delicacy of insects.

The graceful mule deer pick their way down mountain trails in fall, seeking vegetation in the valleys below. High above a few bighorn sheep, laboring among the rocks finding forage, while thousands of American elk (wapiti) move through the park in herds. In autumn, the big-chested bull elks trumpet mightily, the sound echoing and re-echoing as they lead their harems.

There are some birds here in winter, but in summer more than two hundred species from bee-sized hummingbirds to eagles and soaring falcons congregate. This peaceful place even attracts the rare trumpeter swan.

The mountains are hard, crystalline rock, hugging, in part, Cascade Canyon where a trail rims beaver-built ponds and crosses meadows, skirting great slashes of boulders on hillsides. The valley of Jackson Hole is filled with rock and gravel too porous to hold water, and is therefore covered with the tenacious sagebrush, common to semi-desert regions.

The Tetons' beginning was nine million years ago when a chunk of earth was thrust up along the west side of Jackson Hole. The crack in the surface, Teton fault, divided the masses of rock. To the east, they sank, and to the west rose slowly. The high country formed the Tetons, then perhaps some twenty thousand feet above sea level. Erosion worked upon the peaks, sending showers of rock and stone into the valley, then glaciers completed the task in the Ice Age as the sandpaper effect wore away sharp ridges, filling gorges, then water put the finishing touches on these great natural works.

Grand Teton National Park was established in 1929, and in 1950 Congress added another fifty-two square miles to it, the gift of John D. Rockefeller, Jr. It brought the total to about 473 square miles, a spectacular corner of the United States where nature is the great equalizer.

Opposite: Climbers work their way up the Teton Glacier on Grand Teton Mountain. (Bob and Ira Spring Photo)
Overleaf: Jackson Lake is situated at the foot of the Tetons. (Phil McCafferty Photo)

YELLOWSTONE NATIONAL PARK

It is like the creation of the very devil himself: Angry forces of the underworld locked in combat beneath the earth with the sounds and visible fury of their struggle seeping through fissures to enthrall the curious above ground who have come to see what fire and ice have spawned.

This is Yellowstone National Park in the northwest corner of Wyoming (and narrow strips of Idaho and Montana), where nearly all that nature has to offer has been concentrated in a spectacular display unmatched anywhere on earth. Boiling springs, steam vents, mudpots spewing mud and, as a climax, the great geysers hurtling tons of water hundreds of feet skyward — these dot the otherwise pastoral land to make a strangely beautiful if not sometimes forbidding world.

The park's strange landscape had its origin some twenty million years ago when Yellowstone, then a mountain-rimmed basin, became the seat of violent volcanism. Clouds of dust and ash filled the air. Settling shroudlike over the land, it buried entire forests. Fiery cascades of semimolten rock rolled down the mountainsides, and great fissures belched forth enormous volumes of highly fluid lava. Some six hundred cubic miles of this molten rock was spewed out onto the land. The mountain-rimmed basin filled; it was a basin no longer, and Yellowstone became a high plateau.

But a few scars remained, as did a handful of open wounds which could never quite heal because of the cancerous fury far beneath. The heat of these pre-historic volcanoes remains, much like a storage battery to provide power for the sights which greet the visitor today.

Old Faithful is aptly named, for it is prompt, appearing about once an hour, day and night, hurling fifteen thousand gallons of hot water in a single, magnificent unleashing of force. There are few other places in the world where such phenomena exist — New Zealand, Chile and Iceland.

Opposite: Calcium carbonate deposits terrace colorfully at Mammoth Hot Springs, forming a quasi-frozen waterfall. (National Park Service Photo) Right: Trumpeter swans stay at Yellowstone all year because the water is heated from hot springs. (Erwin A. Bauer Photo)

Old Faithful has two hundred cousins at Yellowstone, among them the Riverside, Grotto, Castle and Beehive geysers, all sustained in the same way. Cold water from the long winter's melted snows finds its way through the hard volcanic rock around the geysers. Thousands of feet below the surface it is heated by hot rocks and also by gases and natural steam escaping from still deeper molten rock. Soon the cool water begins to boil, building pressure as steam forms, forcing the water higher into the geyser column. Then as the pressure is relaxed, huge quantities of steam are formed within the underground chambers, forcing the column of water to the surface in a pulsating, continuous finger of dancing liquid, pirouetting on the surface for four or five minutes. Suddenly the mad ballet ends, the crown of vapor floats skyward and the water recedes as the energy of the steam dissipates.

The stories of the early travelers to Yellowstone, such as John Colter in 1807-1808, were looked upon with skepticism. But the tales continued, and finally in 1870 Yellowstone was officially "discovered." Two years later it became the nation's and the world's first national park.

High above much of the park is Yellowstone Lake, a body of water stretching twenty miles in one direction, fourteen in the other. Its mirrorlike surface can be broken into giant whitecaps within minutes as storms blow in from the snow-capped Rockies beyond, or great bolts of lightning are discharged between the surface and the sky.

It seems nothing will change in Yellowstone for the forces of nature are not easily swayed. Here there is no man-made edifice or unnatural changes by machine. There is no skyscraper, except some of rock, or hole torn in the earth, except the slowly evolving depression caused by water and wind today and the volcanoes or glaciers of yesterday. There is peace and ultimate grandeur in Yellowstone, a legacy left by nature and administered for all the heirs of tomorrow.

Left: The American elk (wapiti) is the largest deer in the United States. He makes a far-carrying bugle sound. (Erwin A. Bauer Photo) Opposite: Laced with snow, the dark ridges of the Absaroka Mountains extend for 175 miles into northwestern Wyoming. (Grant Heilman Photo)

GLACIER NATIONAL PARK

Upper St. Mary Lake in Montana is a sphere of blue — a sapphire of water worn like a jewel, mirroring wisps of cotton clouds and wearing the sharp lines of surrounding mountains as the hands upon the face of a clock. The massive peaks, sheer, sharp walls of stone, are the rulers of this empire of trees and water and wildlife, flower-strewn meadows and living glaciers existing almost side by side in paradoxical enjoyment of their environments.

Here there are the seekers of this extraordinary beauty, the "Crown of the Continent," which includes more than a thousand miles of trails which lace through nearly 1,600 square miles of wild loveliness.

The ice-fingers of earth-evolution are not far from the velvety grass spread of hills and valleys sprinkled with summer flowers, one of the four biological life zones found here. Above are the spruce and fir, and surmounting them are subalpine plants, while still farther lie the colors — green, white and pastels — which hint at life in the most improbable places. Snow-capped peaks touch the limits of the sky a mile or more above the looking glasses of over two hundred lakes.

The joyous sound of rushing water fills the spectator's ears, the pounding of diamond-blue streams cascading over moss-strewn stones and the never-ending roar of waterfalls tossing dancing crystals into the air above, defying time to stop their existence.

The geological history of the land is the foundation upon which this extraordinary beauty rests; plants and animals, fish and fowl are here because of the chain of events which evolved to form this panorama, from its rugged peaks mantled with snow to the green spread of meadows and valleys.

The heights arrived when the Rockies came into being sixty million years ago, but while that great stretch of peaks rose, new forces vised this

Opposite: *Flinsch Peak is a cirque caused by ice erosion. (Gene Ahrens Photo) Trick Falls (right) in the Two Medicine area. (Joyce Turvey Photo)*

Canadian-border region, bringing it sharply together, forcing the infant mountains sideways until finally the folded earth broke under the strain. The pressure continued, edging the land to the east for almost forty miles.

Sedimentary layers — silts, sands, clays and muds — started it all a billion or two years ago in the shallow arm of a prehistoric sea. Chemical changes coupled with time and pressure solidified the layers, and they submerged, then emerged.

A million years ago, the valley floors lay beneath great glaciers which relentlessly ground downhill. They gave way years ago to smaller masses of ice, but not before the park's valleys were filled with ice three-fifths of a mile high. Then the earth became warm again, and magical-ly the ice disappeared, then returned in lesser fury to cover the earth once more.

There is still preponderous evidence of the glaciers here, despite the warming trend. Nearly three hundred acres are still covered by Sperry Glacier, about four hundred feet deep, a latter-day, and comparatively miniscule, sample of what helped shape this region. Those flowing rivers of ice of a million years ago grabbed par-ticles of sand and massive boulders, edging them along to rasp at the landscape and form today's rugged spectacle.

The hewn earth is a natural habitat for 57 species of animals and 210 bird species, some of which rest here a day or two twice a year during migration.

Light clouds cover 8,848-foot Mount Grinnell and Grinnell Glacier on the eastern edge of the Continental Divide. (Gene Ahrens Photo)

SAWTOOTH NATIONAL FOREST

"Solitude," according to James Russell Lowell, "is as needful to the imagination as society is wholesome for the character." For people who like solitude, Idaho offers acres of it, particularly in the Sawtooth Wilderness Area, declared such after a long and bitter battle between mine and commercial developers and conservationists. The Sawtooth is located in southern Idaho, the potato capital of the world, and partly in Utah.

The region of natural beauty that is Idaho's pride received Congressional approval as a national recreation area in 1972. An hour's drive north of Sun Valley, it embraces the Sawtooth Primitive Area, over 200,000 acres in the Sawtooth and Boise national forests, where the Salmon River is born in snow crevices and cascading waterfalls. The Sawtooths are the home of deer, elk, mountain goat, bear and mountain lion, and were a special favorite of Gary Cooper and Ernest Hemingway.

The Sawtooths are popular today with hikers, climbers, trail riders and fishermen. In the valley, Redfish Lake, the largest lake, is noted for two species of salmon — the chinook and landlocked kokanee. The visitor center at the lakeshore interprets broad phases of natural and human history, including the lusty mining days of the late nineteenth century. Elsewhere in the recreation area, remains of mining camps — Sawtooth City and Vienna — are being preserved to tell their story for themselves.

Big Redfish Lake is noted for two species of salmon—chinook and landlocked kokanee. (National Forest Service Photo)

CLEARWATER NATIONAL WILD and SCENIC RIVER

From the time of the earliest settlers, America's rivers have been an integral part of our history, serving as avenues of commerce, sources of municipal water, and providers of electric power and irrigation for farmlands. They continue to nourish our growth, but these rivers, once also used for recreation, have become increasingly polluted and stripped of their freshness and appeal by all manner of intrusions.

In an attempt to preserve many tributaries and sections of rivers in an unspoiled condition, a new and different concept of conservation was launched in 1968 with the passage of the National Wild and Scenic Rivers Act. In this act Congress declared: "... That certain selected rivers of the Nation ... shall be preserved in free-flowing condition, and that they and their immediate environments shall be protected ...."

The sparkling waters of the Middle Fork of the Clearwater River in northern Idaho and its tributaries, the Selway and Lochsa rivers, became a part of this system. Within the Clearwater, Bitterroot and Nezperce national forests, the streams are under the management of the U.S. Forest Service. Running westward from the Bitterroot Mountains to the town of Kooskia, the rivers are the most accessible of any in the system. The Lewis and Clark Highway parallels the Middle Fork of the Clearwater and the Lochsa rivers, and another road follows the lower Selway River, but the upper Selway is still quite primitive.

Cutting through heavily forested and partly barren mountains, the rivers alternate from swift rapids to smooth, slow-flowing currents, providing variety for the canoeist or rubber-raft floater. Elk, moose and otters may frequently be observed near the Lewis and Clark Highway, and the Rocky Mountain goat is a common sight in the Black Canyon area.

Among the stately evergreens of Idaho, the Middle Fork of the Clearwater winds its blue waters, rippled white from underwater rocks. (H. Armstrong Roberts Photo)

CRATERS of the MOON NATIONAL MONUMENT

A desolate landscape of unyielding blacks, chocolate-to-golden tans, and sometimes, rusty-reds, has made another world of an eighty-three-square-mile sector of south-central Idaho. Ebony-colored rock rivers, glinting bluish purple in strong sunlight, are guarded by peculiar open cones, startlingly red inside with side slopes of tawny brown shadings.

Characteristics of this strange land on the northern reaches of the Snake River Lava Plain between the Pioneer and the Lost River mountains bear striking resemblance to the craters and darkened valleys of the moon as viewed through telescopes. Therefore, in 1924, when President Coolidge set aside 53,545 acres of this barren wasteland, it was named Craters of the Moon National Monument.

Volcanic eruptions resulting in extensive lava flows during at least three different time periods are responsible for this foreboding wasteland. The molten, gaseous rock killed all growing things in its path, leaving one of the harshest environments known. Time determinations, made from the life span rings of pines found growing in the newest lava flows, indicate the last eruptions ended at least two thousand years ago.

Early westbound settlers avoided the area, but in the 1880's, two venturesome cattlemen, J. W. Powell and Arthur Ferris, explored this wasteland hoping to find a permanent water supply for their livestock. Later studies by the U. S. Geological Survey caused wide-spread interest resulting in the national monument designation.

The era of volcanism responsible for Craters of the Moon perhaps encompassed a million years. Although the monument resembles a gigantic, cataclysmic convolution, most of these lava flows and cinder cones rose through what is called the Great Rift — a fissure in the earth's crust that can be traced through the monument — in relatively mild fashion. Cinder cones, both large and small, show that the eruptions occurred along a definite line pattern.

A marvelous view from atop Big Cinder Butte reveals two distinct forms of basaltic (black) lava involved in these eruptions. The *pahaohoe* (pronounced pah-HO ay-HO-ay) and *aa* (ah-ah) are the two. *Pahoehoe* is a billowy, ropy type of lava having many caverns and covers about half of the monument area. Its shiny blue, glassy crusts make some of the flows darkly beautiful in brilliant sunlight. The ropy, wrinkled surfaces are caused by the hardening of a thin crust on the lava flow while the underlying molten rock continues in motion.

In contrast, the *aa* is rough, jagged and spiny — apparently having the same chemical origin, but made up of a different combination of gas and heat. When it is flowing hot this kind of lava is a doughy mass and escaping gas pulls out stringers of lava, causing the spines. The whole flow resembles slush ice on a river in springtime. Flows of *aa* lava in the monument are twenty-five to one hundred feet thick and some of them extend miles into the plains nearby.

A variety of cinder cones, spatter cones and lava domes are seen in the monument. Cones are formed by lava froth or spray from fire fountains at the time of eruptions. Big Cinder Butte is the finest example in the area, with rich browns and tans and undersides composed of smaller cinders which are sometimes a brilliant brick red.

Spatter cones were built by smaller fire fountains when clots of lava were hurled from the eruption hole and moved so slowly in the air for such short distances that they failed to cool, and thus were literally "spattered" when they landed. Lava domes have smooth domelike shapes rising from ten to fifty feet high in the monument. These interesting formations came from continuous, slow-welling lava from the same vent opening along the Great Rift.

Opposite: One of the strangest landscapes in America is the unearthly wasteland contained in the Craters of the Moon National Monument where volcanic formations, like these black spatter cones, are bounded by distant mountains. (H. Armstrong Roberts Photo)

ROCKY MOUNTAIN NATIONAL PARK

High over the mile-high city of Denver, Colorado, fifty miles to the northwest, is the "roof of America." The four hundred or more square miles of craggy heights which we know as Rocky Mountain National Park, in the Rocky Mountains, contain 107 named peaks over eleven thousand feet in skyward reach.

What has been aptly called an alpine tundra is predominantly a terrain of few trees. Beyond the treeline ranges one third of the park area, with rolling, grassy slopes softening the panoramic onslaught of granite cliffs and spires.

In the two brief months of the highland summer the park is a land of enchantment, the atmosphere heady with the fragrance of tiny alpine wildflowers. In other seasons it is often bleak and desolate, wind-swept, with gales of arctic intensity swirling the snows into multiple hollows and crevices amid great peaks.

Far to the east, breathtakingly beautiful as seen from the uplands, the leveling edges of the Great Plains give one a literal sense of the immensity and variety of our continent. To the north, south and west, the skyline is broken by the serrated crests and other mountain ranges.

This is obviously the prime attraction for visitors: the view, as it were, from the top of our land. Unparalleled in its accessibility, because of the Trail Ridge Road, which winds through these uplands, tourists find themselves positioned, without need for the skill and strain of mountain climbing, at an elevation of 12,183 feet.

Historically, a route roughly following the Trail Ridge Road was used by the Utes and Arapahoes in crossing the Continental Divide. It was called *Taieonbaa*, the "Child's Trail," because it was so steep in places that children had to dismount from their horses and walk.

Archeological research reveals that the Ute-Arapahoe Trail may have been in use for the past eight thousand years.

Unlike many of the Western national parks, there is little historical evidence that the area was extensively used by either Indians or whites in the exploration and winning of the West. Hunting parties from the tribes on either side of the Divide visited the area in summer on hunting trips. Berry-picking and just plain recreation were not unknown in these calming hunts. Trappers assessed the fur-bearing potential of the region — these, the informal explorers, must have been familiar with Longs Peak, awesomely viewed from the plains below. Two more formal parties, Lt. Zebulon Pike in 1806, and Major Stephen H. Long in 1820 — for whom the peak was named — charted the uncharted for future generations.

In 1859 Joel Estes discovered the valley which was to bear his name. He moved his family to the "gorgeous gorge" and thus initiated further settlement of the town and valley now familiar as Estes Park.

The tremendous potential of the expanse of glaciated landscapes, as a national park, was grasped and articulated by surveyor and conservationist Enos Mills. At the tender age of sixteen he had built a home in the Longs Peak valley in 1886. In 1891 he had filled his spirit enduringly working with a survey party in the Yellowstone. With a ferocity born of dedication to, and belief in conservation, he fought unceasingly for the ultimate establishment of Rocky Mountain National Park in 1915. Mills died in 1922, but some of his statements seem to have a touch of the immortality of the Rockies he loved and fought for: "Room — glorious room," he wrote, "room in which to find ourselves."

Opposite: Hallett Peak is one of 107 named peaks over eleven thousand feet in the Park. (National Park Service Photo)

ARCHES NATIONAL PARK

The Colorado Plateau contains the most colorful, varied, sculptured land on the face of the earth, and Arches is one of its masterpieces. In this 137-square-mile national park in southeastern Utah, sedimentary rock, formed in lakes and floods before the memory of man, has been shaped gloriously by the carving tools of wind-blown sand, frost and moisture. The result is a superb display of eroded formations that together form a collection of stone arches, windows, spires and pinnacles unequalled in this country.

Established in 1929, the size of Arches, then a monument, doubled in 1969 when President Lyndon B. Johnson signed an enlargement proclamation. Three years later Congress declared the area a national park.

Inside the park are eighty-eight natural arches carved from Entrada sandstone, layered above the hues of Navajo and Carmel sandstone formations. These huge sandstone masterpieces, formed near the confluence of the Green and Colorado rivers, are surrounded by picturesque canyons, tall, snow-capped mountains in the distance, and an azure desert sky floating above the red, yellow, buff and brown layers of rock.

Perhaps the most fascinating of these arches is Landscape Arch. Thought to be the longest natural span in the world, it is 291 feet across and towers to a height of 120 feet, with the smallest point in the arch now eroded to less than six feet in diameter.

Other splendid natural arches in all stages of erosion may be seen in the park with rock strata standing out in bold colors. These Jurassic Age formations begin near the valley floors with the Navajo Formation sweeping upward in a rounded, sloping mass of light-colored sandstone. In this area, the Navajo Formation has become pock-marked allowing enough silt to accumulate for rooting juniper trees, which seem to grow from solid rock.

Above the Navajo is the Carmel Foundation, identified by its thin strata of red bands of wavy sedimentation. Above the Carmel is the layer of Entrada sandstone where most of the arches have been formed.

Double Arch displays twin bows, a perforated fin and a pothole formation, and is located in the Windows section, an area ideal for studying the rock strata. (Utah Highway Department Photo)

CAPITOL REEF NATIONAL PARK

The violent upthrust of multicolored barrier cliffs stretching one hundred miles across the south-central Utah desert looks like a huge ocean wave suspended between the Fremont River and its two tributaries. These interruptions in the striking shale and sandstone escarpments resemble the clustered buildings of a city — hence the appellation Capitol Reef given to this area by Captain John C. Fremont, who viewed the area from Thousand Lake Mountain in 1854.

This magnificent escarpment is the western face of a folding of the earth's crust that occurred in some ancient upheaval. Major John Wesley Powell, a geologist who first explored this region in 1869, called this upthrust the Waterpocket Fold. Capitol Reef National Park preserves a quarter of a million acres of the most picturesque parts of this geological museum. Here the term "paintbrush of nature" takes on a special meaning with vermilion-hued shale layers and walls of glowing pink and white mixing with splatters of orange and ocher. The brilliance deepens to "a land of horizontal rainbows" as day wears on.

The surging and folding of the earth's surface caused the eastern segment of the fold to top the western side and erosion has exposed the stratified crust formation. Cliffs range from one thousand to two thousand feet high, making an almost impassable barrier to crossing the desert from west to east. At the base of the cliffs natural cisterns called potholes catch and retain the only fresh water to be found for many miles across the desert. These water catchments caused Powell to call it the Waterpocket Fold.

Petroglyphs chipped into the walls of the scarp or in caves hollowed into the sandstone provide a record of prehistoric eras. Small bands of Indians grew corn on the valley floor, and artifacts, including bone tools, pottery stone implements and rough fabrics, are kept in a museum at the park's visitor center.

The peculiar geographic isolation of Capitol Reef caused it to be one of the last areas of Utah to be explored and settled. It was, however, scarcities of both water and arable land that kept settlement sparse.

Thin soils in the valleys and gorges, plus the paucity of rainfall, have maintained Capitol Reef's ecology as a typical sample of the plants and wildlife of the Colorado Plateau. Pinyon-juniper communities, along with sage, saltbush and squawbush are dominant. Deer, foxes, bobcats and porcupines as well as small rodents and numerous lizards comprise the wildlife. Upland species of birds also inhabit the area.

At Capitol Gorge early settler Cutler Behunin decided to make a wagon trail in 1880. He entered the gorge with tools and wagons, but eight days later he had progressed only three and a half miles. Yet until recent years, his trail was the only traverse of the fold in that area.

The loneliness of Capitol Reef is captured by the view across the desert to the Henry Mountains in the distance. This was the last major mountain range to be named in the United States.

Isolated and desolate, this part of the mile-high land of southern Utah was first set aside in 1937. In 1969 President Lyndon B. Johnson extended it by more than 200,000 acres to preserve the most spectacular parts of the Waterpocket Fold. In late 1972, Congress changed the status of the area from a monument to a national park. A visitor center, public camping and picnic areas, plus two private motel and lodge areas inside the park, assist travelers in seeing this out-of-the-way sector of North America.

Capitol Reef today remains almost exactly as it was when geologist C. E. Dutton said of it a century ago: "The colors are such as no pigments can portray. They are deep, rich and variegated; and so luminous are they, that light seems to flow or shine out of the rock rather than to be reflected from it."

Opposite: A great dome of erosion-sculpted rock towers above a river bed. (Utah Highway Department Photo)

CEDAR BREAKS NATIONAL MONUMENT

A gigantic natural amphitheater, carved from multihued stone, slopes steeply westward from two-mile high Markagunt Plateau in southwestern Utah. This is a spectacular example of the deterioration of limestone formations uptilted by ancient shiftings of the earth's crust. The gently rolling rim of this grotesquely eroded area is covered by a verdant growth of trees interspersed with lush meadows which display mountain wildflowers soon after the retreat of melting snow. Color, both from various metallic mixes in the limestone and from the lush plant growth, is probably the dominant characteristic of this dramatic area only two and a half miles from Brian Head Peak, the highest point in southwestern Utah.

Early Mormon settlers called the area "breaks" or "badlands." That early name became Cedar Breaks because settlers mistakenly identified the mountain juniper of the area as cedar. This scenic display of erosion became part of Dixie National Forest in 1905, and about ten square miles was established as Cedar Breaks National Monument in 1933. From the rim of the plateau at 10,300 to 10,400 feet above sea level, the amphitheater drops almost half a mile to its lowest point.

Bold rock shapes and cliffs carved from stone layers two thousand feet thick are revealed from outlook points along the rim. Sidewalls are furrowed, corroded and broken into massive ridges that seem to radiate from the center like spokes of a wheel. This geologic display of color starts at the top with white or orange limestone ranging downward through rose and coral tints. Yellows, lavenders and even purples and chocolate hues are seen in many sections of the prodigious natural bowl. The Indians called it "circle of painted cliffs." An artist once counted forty-seven different tints in the stones of the monument.

Patches of snow mix with the golden orange on the walls to give an abstract effect. (James Fain Photo)

WHITE SANDS NATIONAL MONUMENT

White Sands National Monument preserves the most spectacular part of the world's largest gypsum dune field — great rolling hills of dazzling white sand that provide a severe environment for the animals and plants which have managed to survive in it. The monument is set in the Tularosa Basin of southern New Mexico that extends for over a hundred miles between mountains and highlands, the remnants of a plateau.

These mountains, including the forested Sacramentos to the east and rugged San Andres to the west, contain massive layers of gypsum rock that seasonal rains and melting snows have been eroding for centuries. Dissolved gypsum is eventually carried to Lake Lucero, the lowest part of the basin at the southern end, where the warm sun and dry winds evaporate the lake, leaving it a gypsum-crystal encrusted marsh much of the year. Gypsum also lies beneath the basin floor, evidence that it was once part of the high plateau around it. Capillary action draws the gypsum-laden underground water to the surface which, after evaporation, leaves extensive alkali flats north of the lake. Persistent, scouring winds from the southwest disintegrate the crystals in the lake bed and the alkali flats into brilliant white grains of sand, pile them into dunes and push the dunes across the landscape as new ones are constantly formed.

The dune area is now about thirty miles long and twelve miles wide. Dune peaks are as high as fifty feet.

Yet life survives, including over a hundred species of hardy plants. Even on the barren alkali flats some vegetation holds on with amazing tenacity — such as clumps of pickleweed or iodine bush. Sparse ground cover between the marginal dunes is made up primarily of delicate purple sand verbena, pink centauriums and rice grass.

The groundwater only three or four feet below the surface gives White Sands an advantage over most other dune areas, but it is only a slight one, for few plants can use the gypsum-laden water. Among those that can absorb it are the skunkbush sumac (squawbush), soaptree yucca, shrubby pennyroyal, rubber rabbit brush and cottonwood tree.

Few animals live in the sands. Coyotes, occasional foxes, and the skunks, porcupines and gophers sometimes seen in the dunes come from the surrounding area. To avoid these predators, two species unique to White Sands have evolved white coloration to help protect them. A small pocket mouse is seldom seen because he is nocturnal. In contrast with this white pocket mouse, the red hills nearby contain a pocket mouse that is a rusty color, and in the black lava beds north of the sands is a black race. The small white lizard can frequently be seen scampering over the sand during the day. It has no external ear openings and has overlapping scales on its upper lip to keep sand out of its mouth.

Established in 1933, the monument has an eight-mile scenic drive into the heart of the dunes. Near the end of the drive is an immense picnic area with fireplaces and shaded tables, but there is no campground. Vehicles are restricted to roads because they can easily bog down if they are driven on the dunes. However, a brief walk to the top of one of the great dunes can bring you an exhilarating experience in a sea of glistening sand and sky, silent except for the relentless wind.

Opposite: The marginal areas of White Sands support a few vigorous plants like the hybrid varieties of woody-stemmed yucca. (Bill Jack Rodgers Photo)

BIG BEND NATIONAL PARK

The Great River, the Rio Grande, running a fairly straight southeast course, edging the United States and Mexico across the Chihuahua desert, suddenly bends around to its left and cuts to the north past the Chisos Mountains for a total of 107 miles. And before it turns south again it puts a heart-shaped lower boundary on Big Bend National Park.

Here is the wilderness. Here is the unexplored. Here is the West (with a capital letter) in all of its desert and mountain and storybook wildness.

In this day of overcrowding, bustle and hustle and nudging neighbors, parts of Big Bend National Park, which is within three hundred miles of El Paso, Texas, and four hundred miles of San Antonio, are still not fully explored. Parts of it are so untouched by this world of the twentieth century that a vacationer can ride his horse out from the comforts of a modern resort area and within an hour feel that he is alone in a world, uninhabited, untouched, and perhaps, before he himself looked upon it, unseen.

Even the suddenly green pockets of lush cotton-wood-lined oases along the river's edge seem like gentle guests (rather than settlers) of the sweeping mesa and rolling mountain land that tolerate their being there with the preoccupied hospitality of a host who has great matters on his mind.

This area has never been an easy one to know. It grudgingly permitted some acquaintanceship, but never sought or welcomed friendship; and it never offered itself or its resources to explorers, ranches, miners or farmers. It wasn't until 1899 that anyone made a trip of record around the "big bend" of the Rio Grande. Others may have gone there before Robert T. Hill and five companions explored it for the Geological Survey in 1850, but the others went to raid, to smuggle or to hide.

Train robbers, bank robbers, American fugitives and Mexican bandits slipped in and out of the area as they slipped in and out of the history of the outlaw-gunman West. Here, as late as 1916, Mexican bandits, possibly some of Pancho Villa's men, invaded the United States.

But today the men of violence are gone. Today, if the visitor hears rustling in the underbrush, it is probably not a cattle rustler but a javelina or a mule deer, a cougar or a white-tailed deer.

In the middle of the park, the Chisos Mountains rise up like a string of fortified castles set to hold back the advance of the hordes of sage and cactus on the desert floor. The mountains throw their forest troops into battle lines against the invaders. In the front rank are the stunted oak and drooping juniper, and on the higher ground, the pinyon pine, Douglas fir and ponderosa pine.

The name of these mountains, "Chisos," is hard to translate. Part Indian, part Spanish, it carries the idea of ghostly wonder or enchantment in and out of both languages. And these mountains speak the mystery that surrounds Big Bend National Park.

Looking south from their south rim, a visitor knows in his mind that he is looking towards Mexico, but in the clear bright air and the isolated silence of a seemingly never-ending distance his heart begins to feel that he is looking over the edge of the world itself. He feels for just a moment on the edge of time itself so that, as a local saying has it, standing here on the side of the mountains of mystery, "on a clear day, you can see clear into the day after tomorrow."

Flowers begin to bloom in the lowlands in late February but do not reach the mountain heights until May. Spring also brings occasional "northers," sudden storms that bring chill winds and often dust. The mountains are particularly attractive in the summer when temperatures in the desert and valley hover around one hundred degrees. With the end of autumn — warm, gentle and delicately colored — comes the sparkling clean air of winter. Once or twice a year snow comes to the mountains, but usually in winter the heights are merely brisk while the canyons remain comfortably warm during the day.

Opposite: The century plant, which blooms each decade, in the Chisos Mountains (National Park Service Photo)

SUNSET CRATER
NATIONAL MONUMENT

In 1065, one year before William the Conqueror and his bands of Normans landed on the British Isles, a few farming Indians called Sinagua lived in the present Little Colorado River basin in north-central Arizona near the San Francisco Peaks. Because of the lack of moisture, these people located their farmlands near the edge of old cinder beds which had the best soils for crops.

One day they were startled by a sudden volcanic eruption in their fields. A small earthquake caused a minor break in the earth's crust. Steam and gases hissed from the hole, and as the vent grew, the increased pressure ripped chunks of rock and dirt from the edge and sides.

The Indians, doubtless fearful of this evidence of some god's anger, must have fled for safety. Turning around, they would probably have seen the pieces of red-hot lava blowing from the eruption vent and a huge black dust cloud blocking the sun from view.

Heavier particles, cinders and lava built up around the hole, forming a small cone which continued to grow as days passed and the eruptions increased with intensity.

For six months this activity continued as explosive outbreaks were interspersed with outpourings of molten lava from new vents near the base of the cone, creating rivers of lava which hardened in mid-flow. Steaming spatter cones and crusted lava lagoons were formed, and the cinder cone reached a height of a thousand feet before activity slackened.

For years after, hot springs and vapors seeped out from fumaroles around the main vent, and minerals from the vapors stained the cinders at the crater's rim so that the summit seemed to glow with the colors of a sunset.

Gradually vegetation took a tenuous hold in the immediate vicinity of the cone, and some of the hardier Indians moved back to their ash-covered lands, finding that the volcanic materials held the moisture in the soil, and crops grew tall with a much greater yield than before. Word of this productive farmland spread and the Sinagua area became a melting pot of Indian culture — Pueblo, Hohokam, Mogollon and Cohonimo. Continuous farming and winds, however, soon removed the protective layer of ash, and archeologists believe, by 1225, only a few Indians remained in the region and villages were left to the elements.

This volcanic cone is now the Sunset Crater National Monument. The sparse vegetation con-

Sparse vegetation, like the gnarled ponderosa pines and aspens above, has taken hold on the foot of Sunset Crater's lava cone. (H. Armstrong Roberts Photo)

sists mainly of dwarf ponderosa pine and small quaking aspen trees.

The monument, a short distance north of Flagstaff, has a visitor center, and an eighteen-mile road connects Sunset Crater with Wupatki National Historical Monument, where the ruins of the Indian villages have been preserved.

Sunset Crater today is much like it was centuries ago; the fumaroles and spatter cones look like they have barely had time to cool from the violence that formed them.

Opposite: The mile-deep Grand Canyon exposes two billion years of geologic history. After a summer rainstorm, a rainbow bends into the canyon passing a ponderosa pine standing on the rim. (Fred H. Ragsdale Photo, FPG) Above: After a passing rain storm that cooled the endless hot buttes and precipices, clouds rise above the North Rim. (David Muench Photo)

GRAND CANYON NATIONAL PARK

The wind blows gently down this vast wound in the earth, rippling the surface of its creative force, the river, and carrying occasional small puffs of red dust from the awesome walls. The breeze wanes and the eerie silence fans out in four directions, held captive within the impenetrable fortress nature spent nine million years to create.

The Grand Canyon is true to its name, yet a mere, momentary glance prods the beholder's mind, searching for a word more impressive than "Grand." The majestic, water-wrought stone sculpture in Arizona is 217 miles long, averages a mile deep and spreads nine miles across in panorama of pastels, each a page in the book of the canyon's continuing evolution.

In places where the bottom can be reached, the long hike or ride on muleback gradually unfolds in a geological layer cake — gray limestone walls formed when a long-forgotten sea shimmered in the prehistoric sunlight; green shale holding primitive fossils; pastel layer upon pastel layer, until finally millions of years have been passed in a drop of three-fifths of a mile. In the Inner Gorge are sheer walls growing progressively darker as they plunge toward the rushing Colorado River, walls so ancient they were formed before life on the earth.

The river is still building the Grand Canyon, widening it and deepening it an unmeasurable, infinitesimal fraction of an inch each year. Until the closure of Glen Canyon Dam in 1963, the pulsating red torrent of water carried half a million tons of soil downstream each day, each abrasive bit gently, imperceptibly wearing away at the captive walls, loosening other particles in the interminable process of erosion. Today it carries approximately one-sixth as much sediment.

In 1869 its vastness lured John Wesley Powell, the great explorer, here to lead a long and daring expedition through the treacherous canyons and gorges. The Spanish conquistadores stood upon its edge in the mid-1500's, and American trappers visited it in the eighteenth century, but it remained for Powell to conquer the Colorado.

To Powell, the dangerous trip was a labor of unbridled joy. "Past these towering monuments, past these mounted billows of orange sandstone, past these oak-set glens, past these fern-decked alcoves, past these mural curves, we glide hour after hour, stopping now and then as our attention is arrested by some new wonder," Powell wrote.

The spectacle of the canyon from the air is indescribable; flat stretches of unbroken stone suddenly turning ninety degrees and dropping thousands of feet to the silvery knife of water appearing as a line of indolent mercury beneath the noon sun.

To those who find their greatest appreciation of the canyon from within it, rather than standing on the rims and looking below, Theodore Roosevelt was moved to say when the century was only three years old: "In the Grand Canyon, Arizona has a natural wonder which, so far as I know, is in kind absolutely unparalleled .... I hope you will not have a building of any kind . . . or anything else to mar the wonderful grandeur, the sublimity, the great loneliness and the beauty of the canyon. Leave it as it is. You cannot improve on it. The ages have been at work on it, and man can only mar it."

While snow falls on the rim, the temperature may be fifty degrees at the bottom of the canyon. (David Muench Photo)

Zabriskie Point in California's Death Valley lies in an ancient lake bed into which silt was washed. (FPG Photo)

DEATH VALLEY NATIONAL MONUMENT

Heat waves shimmer in the scorching sun as it beats down upon the flats and crags of this barren valley situated between severe mountain ridges rising from a distant desert. It is a heartless master, this valley, unchanged by the softening touch of time. Man's efforts to tame this wilderness seem puny, dwarfed by heaps of lava, burst stone and many-hued clays cast up from beneath the earth's crust in some ancient cataclysm.

Indians who once dwelled in nearby mountains and attempted to harvest a little food from the sparse vegetation called the valley *tomesha*, meaning "red earth," because it yielded a fire-colored clay that warriors used to produce war-paint for their bodies. Sourdough mountain men claimed the Indian word meant "ground afire." But the name that finally attached itself unshakeably to this harsh valley in California is Death Valley.

The name is inappropriate, for this is a land of light, color and considerable beauty. Each shift of light, shadow or perspective casts a different spell because of the infinite variations of color, form and texture.

Out on the broad mud flats and sand dunes, as well as in the specialized ecological communities of cacti, arrowbush and mesquite brush, the life cycles of birds, plants, animals and insects continue in historic patterns. The plants are capable of withstanding the scorching heat and drought through use of peculiar narrowed leaves, broad, deep root systems and unusual seeding methods.

Cloudbursts are a dangerous summer phenomenon in the monument despite the mountains that serve as a barrier to Pacific Ocean moisture. High rising thunderheads occasionally dump torrents of rain in the mountains and create flash floods.

These flash floods cause a rushing wall of water to race down the narrow twisting canyons. The pressure of the water carries huge boulders, silt, gravel and chunks of mountainside with the flood. Suddenly, the gorge opens into the broad valley and the flood waters discharge their load of rocks and silt in a gentle incline at the mouth of the canyon.

The erosion caused by these pell-mell floods from the mountains have gradually filled the valley with silt and rock particles. There is nearly as much "fill" below the surface of the valley now as there is height to the mountain ridges above. Bedrock has been estimated to be nine thousand feet below the surface.

From Aguereberry Point and from Dante's View in the eastern heights, the Devil's Golf Course in the valley below looks like a smooth salt flat. But at floor level one realizes the "flat" consists of crystalline salt which remains when water seeps up to the ground's surface, evaporates and leaves spiked pinnacles as much as two feet high. As the salt pinnacles form, a breaking sound is clearly discernible in the heating and cooling of the valley floor.

Although austere and awesome, Death Valley National Monument has a strong attraction for both naturalists and historians. Here, evidence of the ebullience of the frontier period remains alongside the harsh terrain that appears to threaten the fragile beauty of the isolated patches of wildflowers. However, this strange and foreboding landscape with its mysterious beauty makes an impression on the senses and the imagination that is as enduring as the valley itself.

Aguereberry Point was named for a prospector of the '49 goldrush. (H. Armstrong Roberts Photo)

71

JOSHUA TREE
NATIONAL MONUMENT

Those trees that grow up, down and out in every possible direction are called Joshua trees, said to have been named by the Mormons who saw the crooked, asymmetrical branches as a symbol pointing to the promised land they were seeking, just as the Biblical Joshua pointed the way into the promised land of the Israelites.

In spite of its prickly appearance, the Joshua tree is not a cactus, but a kind of yucca *(Yucca brevifolia)* a member of the greatly varied lily family, and is one of the most spectacular plants of the Southwestern deserts. They grow mostly in southern California, but are also found in a few areas of Nevada, Utah and Arizona. The Joshua tree may attain a height of forty feet and during March and April bears creamy white blossoms in clusters eight to fourteen inches long at the ends of the branches. However, every tree does not bloom every year.

The Joshua tree is often confused with the Mojave yucca (or Spanish dagger) whose leaves are much longer than the Joshua's and also grows at lower elevations. Joshua trees are normally found between three thousand and five thousand feet.

Its sharp, ten-inch-long leaves grow in clusters and when they die, they droop downward and dry into thornlike needles. The branches' strange contortions are caused by the death of the terminal buds after they blossom. Thus each elbow of the crooked arms was at one time the end of the branch where the blossoms died. The twisted arms are also caused by the yucca boring beetle: the tree builds a material over the hole made by the insect, forcing the branch to grow in a different direction.

One of the best stands of Joshua trees in the world is the focus of Joshua Tree National Monument, one hundred miles east of Los Angeles. Located on the border of the California Mojave (mo-HA-vee) and Colorado deserts, the monument, established in 1936, is rich in species of cacti and other desert plant life.

It is phenomenal how these plants survive in the desert with its extreme heat and lack of rain. They give themselves plenty of room to develop extensive root systems, some of which may reach fifty feet from the trunk. The little moisture they do receive — eight or ten inches a year — is strictly rationed by the use of thin, hard bark with few pores to let the moisture escape, or soft, spongy bark which holds water inside.

Jumping cholla (CHOH-ya), also called teddy-bear cholla, is quite conspicuous along the Cholla Cactus Garden Trail in the center of the monument. It is considered the most handsome of the cactus family, but it has many sharp, barbed spines which can easily penetrate the skin. Its name is based on the impression that the spines jump out at anyone who gets too close. The cholla are more friendly to animals, and cactus wrens build their nests in their branches, even adding extra spines for safety against predators. Lizards, crickets, mice and snakes also find haven in jumping cholla.

The short, flat cactus with the magenta blossoms visible in the monument is called beaver tail cactus. Although this plant looks quite smooth from a distance, it has many sharp, tiny spines which readily penetrate the skin.

Most of the monument's animals are nocturnal, but antelope ground squirrels scurry over the sands in the hottest of temperatures. Coyotes are often seen prowling at the outskirts of the campgrounds, but the largest mammal, the desert bighorn sheep, is only occasionally observed.

The brownish kangaroo rats have become so adapted to the dry environment that they can go through their entire lives without ever taking a drink of water. They manufacture water out of their staple diet of dry seeds, grain, and some foliage.

The most commonly seen reptile is the side-blotched lizard (little brown uta), one of many species of lizards in the area. One of the largest, the chuckwalla, can be observed basking on warm rocks in the cooler mornings and evenings. Most of the 250 species of birds that have been sighted in the monument are migrants, and those that remain the year round are usually found near oases.

The outstanding scenic point is Salton View at 5,185 feet. Here in one sweep is an impressive panorama of deserts, valleys and mountains, from the hot, barren Salton Sea, 241 feet below sea level, to the snow-capped summits of San Jacinto and San Gorgonio Peaks, both above ten thousand feet. Thus, Joshua Tree country is also a land of contrasts.

Mormons called this species of yucca the Joshua tree because the branches seemed to point to the promised land. (Ken Short Photo)

REDWOOD NATIONAL PARK

Along the coast of northern California stand some of the oldest living things on earth. In this redwood country there are groves of giant trees which were growing during the Golden Age of ancient Greece.

In order to save as many of these groves as possible for posterity, conservationists in 1918 formed the Save-the-Redwoods League and began a campaign for a national park in northern California. Exactly fifty years later, in 1968 — after a series of stormy battles — their goal was finally realized. Embracing fifty-seven thousand acres of redwoods, bluffs and beaches, Redwood National Park also includes thirty continuous miles of beautiful California coastline. Within the boundaries are three state parks — Jedediah Smith Redwoods, Del Norte Coast Redwoods and Prairie Creek Redwoods — created earlier through the efforts of the Save-The-Redwoods League. These areas have been transferred to the park service and become integral parts of the national park.

Once growing the entire length of the Pacific coast from Oregon to the Big Sur peninsula, coast redwoods are now confined to relatively small areas, and some of these last groves are being logged as these words are written. There are also private landholdings within the park itself which will be logged unless they are added to the park; one hopes these areas will also be preserved in the near future to protect the ecology of the fragile watersheds.

The redwood is a living relic of the past. Redwood fossils have been found in Texas, Pennsylvania, Wyoming and even along the Bering Sea in Alaska. Redwoods once grew in Europe until an ice sheet forced them into the Mediterranean. In central China there are hundreds of what are called Dawn Redwoods, deciduous redwoods that have survived millions of years of floods, fires, droughts and ice.

The coast redwood's scientific name is *Sequoia sempervirens*. Sequoia comes from the Cherokee Indian, Sequoyah, who invented an Indian alphabet and taught his people to read and write; *sempervirens* means evergreen.

The redwood forest ecosystem is a special plant community adapted to the drainage, soil, relatively moderate temperatures and the abundant rain and fog found here — an annual rainfall of a hundred inches is not uncommon. Dominated by the large coast redwood, this ecosystem has an understory thick with smaller trees and shrubs, including flowering rhododendron, huckleberry, salmonberry and azalea. The forest floor, deep with redwood needles and other natural litter, is often out of sight under a cover of ferns.

Numerous streams provide a variation in plant life. Inland forest borders are dry from May through October and consequently have different kinds of vegetation, especially oaks and alders. Along the coast, moisture is so abundant that the redwoods must share the ground with hemlock, spruce, fir and cedar.

Wildlife is plentiful. One of the last surviving California herds of Roosevelt elk can be seen in the open meadows or on the coast. Also present are black-tailed deer, squirrels, foxes, bobcats, chipmunks, raccoons, beavers and river otters. Birds include Steller's jays, grouse, pileated woodpeckers, Western robins and various kinds of thrushes. The streams support a large population of salmon and trout.

The north coastal scrub ecosystem takes over as the forest thins on approaches to the cliffs and scoops in the coastline. This narrow strip is influenced by almost constant salty winds, rocky soils and poor drainage. Low-growing trees, woody shrubs and herbaceous plants dominate here.

The marine and shore ecosystem is fairly typical of the Pacific Northwest Coast. Offshore rocks are havens for seabirds, seals and sea lions, and migrating whales are often observed near the coast. Tidepools and saltwater and freshwater marshes have abundant animal life, and the sandy beaches and dunes are constantly renewed by the ocean's currents.

Opposite: Walking among towering redwood trees is a memorable experience. (Howard King Photo)

YOSEMITE NATIONAL PARK

The dawn sun lies poised over Yosemite National Park, then the murmuring thunder of Bridalveil Creek seems to bring forth the hushed melody of the early morning wind blowing through spires of the groves of sequoias and evergreens as life stirs in this idyllic retreat in the High Sierra of California.

The wonders of Yosemite range from the awesome crash of water to canyons far below to the pastoral silence of flower-flocked meadowlands.

Congress saw its great beauty in 1864, and granted it to the State of California. In 1890 the national park was created around this Yosemite Grant. California ended its control of the grant in 1905, turning it back over to the Federal Government to form an enlarged national park of nearly 1,200 square miles.

Water shaped Yosemite, and still is slowly wearing away rock as it must, seeking the lower levels and carrying with it bits of stone and vegetable matter, endlessly creating. The Upper Yosemite Fall drops 1,430 feet, and the Lower a bit less than a fourth of that. Water cascades with a roar over the top of cliffs for a total drop of 2,425 feet from the crest of the Upper Fall to the base of the Lower.

Not all is the sound and fury of nature. There is solitude in Yosemite to be found in her stands of sequoias. Growing silently, contributing to its grandeur, are the park's incense-filled forests of pine, fir, cedar and oak, providing habitat for band-tailed pigeons, pygmy owls, chipmunks and squirrels.

In spring, there is a flood of color — brilliant yellows and soft blues with the dark green of the conifers filling the eye with the splendor of an untouched land. In winter, the high country is forbidding when giant snows fill the land, only to melt into the trickle of mountain streams which become the raging torrent to start life anew in this land of ten thousand wonders.

Bridalveil Fall, in Yosemite, drops between the Cathedral Rocks 620 feet. (FPG Photo)

DEVILS POSTPILE NATIONAL MONUMENT

The tremendous gray-brown mass of columnar stones, rising vertically from among the lush forests and wildflower meadows of California's high Sierra Nevada, resembles a pipe organ from some legendary age of giants. On a talus slope at the foot of this perpendicular facing are fragmented sections of polygonal columns strewn in a jumbled mass as though the giant, tiring of his prodigious toy, had smashed parts of it in a fit of anger.

Here 7,600 feet above sea level, this convoluted mass is the remnant of a million-year-old volcanic eruption. Dominating the surrounding forests and meadows, the entire formation is approximately nine hundred feet long, and as much as two hundred feet high. The columns are from forty to sixty feet tall.

This geological oddity, one of the most remarkable of its kind in North America, is formed of dark, basaltic lava flows, and is included in a one-by-three-mile area set aside in 1911 as Devils Postpile National Monument. It lies between Yosemite and Sequoia national parks on the John Muir Trail. Included in the monument are part of the Middle Fork of the San Joaquin River valley and Rainbow Falls on this river. Soda Spring — carbonated by carbon dioxide gases escaping into the water source from volcanic activity deep in the earth — also is in the monument, upstream from the Devils Postpile formation.

Volcanic eruptions higher in the Sierra Nevada, to the east of the monument, caused the original flow more than 900,000 years ago. As the mass cooled, the lava cracked (something like drying mud) into forms with three to seven sides. These forms extend from the surface downward into the mass, and seen in cross section, they resemble columns.

Several times in the last million years, glaciers, some as much as a thousand feet thick, flowed down the river valley and quarried away much of the lava deposits, including one side of the postpile. Only the more resistant columns, the ones seen today, remained standing. Most of the columns are vertical, but some are slanted and others curved, probably due to slight differences in composition, thickness and cooling rates. The tops of the remaining columns were exposed at right angles to the glacial movement and were polished to a high sheen, giving the appearance of a mosaic. In most places, however, they have been roughed by weathering during the time since the last glacial period.

Near upper reaches of the monument is a pumice flat which originated in the post-glacial era. This rock will float on water, but as it powders, it creates a fine dust. In some areas of the monument, this pumice is crumbly, making the footing difficult as one walks about. Some evidence of recent volcanic activity such as bubbly, hot springs are found nearby.

Rainbow Falls on the Middle Fork of the San Joaquin River, about two miles downstream from the Devils Postpile, provides a thrilling view of this rushing river as it plunges over a precipice 140 feet into a deep green pool below. At the foot of the falls are clumps of willows, Western white pine, hemlocks, alders, and numerous wildflowers.

A campground, open from mid-June to October, is maintained at the National Park Service ranger station in the monument. Two miles away from the postpile, at Reds Meadow, supplies, cabins, meals and both saddle and pack horses are available.

The awesome natural forces that sculpted this geometrically shaped Devils Postpile and the volcanic rubble from lava flows torn by glaciation make this monument a mecca for scientists and those interested in natural wonders.

*Devils Postpile is a sector of huge basalt pillars, with four to seven
sides each, left standing in the Middle Fork of the San Joaquin valley after a glacier
removed the greater part of an ancient lava deposit. (H. Armstrong Roberts Photo)*

Nestled among decaying litter of pine and fir needles
is the snow plant, a bright saprophyte. (John Kauffmann Photo, National Park Service)

SEQUOIA and KINGS CANYON NATIONAL PARKS

The tree is king here, peering down over a majestic domain of gray granite mountains, deep forests and valleys making a harsh but welcoming slash in the landscape. It stands, holding court over a seemingly untouched panorama, beginning beyond one horizon and going past the other.

This tree is the largest living thing in the world — rivaling the age of any tree or other plant known — the sequoia, gently elbowing aside white firs and sugar pines, its cinnamon-red bark and pointed needles quite unchanged from the time when frightening creatures rumbled the earth with their ponderous tread.

One can count nearly four thousand years since some of them were born, and science believes none has died simply because of old age. They usually find their life-giving roots exposed by slow erosion, perhaps nature's way to return organic material to the soil. Then they topple and

die with a crash, to lie fallen beside other warriors fighting the long battle against time in Sequoia and Kings Canyon national parks in California.

There are more than 1,300 square miles in the two parks, starting at the foothills of the San Joaquin Valley and reaching toward the crest of the High Sierra. It is some six thousand feet above sea level here, and the altitude makes the giant sequoias seem all the more regal.

The nucleus of a visit here is the General Sherman Tree, largest of all living things on earth, towering more than 272 feet above the ground and measuring more than 35 feet across the base. Because it is hard to imagine such a tree, perhaps this helps: The trunk alone weighs approximately 1,450 tons and has 50,010 cubic feet of wood, enough to build about forty homes. The General Grant is only five feet shorter and contains only a bit less wood.

This is a rugged land, existing almost as a separate entity from the rest of the West. Beyond the Giant Forest, named by that great, Scots-born naturalist, John Muir, is the Sierra Nevada's high country, a vast, tilted block on the earth where snowcapped peaks — crowned by Mount Whitney, the highest mountain in the United States outside of Alaska — rise to more than fourteen thousand feet to cast giant shadows on glacial valleys and ice-formed lake basins.

Great canyons are incised upon the landscape, among the deepest to be found in the United States. Gorges along the middle and south forks of the Kings River are more than a mile deep, their steep sides forming a canyon between the great peaks and the roaring waters tumbling over time-polished stones below.

Here there are valleys, miles long and a half-mile wide, created when small streams grew larger and carried infinitesimal bits of stone with their downhill fury, then finally hewn to shape by vast fields of ice jamming their depths.

Some of these valleys are covered with forests of ponderosa pine, incense-cedar and white fir, towering above blue lupine waving in the summer breeze. Deer, bear and bobcats graze and hunt among the trees. Birds flutter against wind gusts, then swoop earthward to grasp an insect in their beaks, and retreat to the forest a few wing flaps beyond to enjoy their meal and perhaps sing of triumph.

High above — nearly two miles on top of the level of the sea — is a mountain wilderness dotted with glacial lakes mirroring the sun and its spectacular surroundings.

Magnificent, even in winter when snow festoons the giant sequoias and fills the dips and small valleys, there is no word that does justice to the parks and their environs.

Although the General Grant Tree is the second largest of all sequoias, it is still one hundred feet higher than Niagara Falls. (Gene Ahrens Photo)

In Olympic, the highest amount of annual rainfall in the United States creates yellow-green rain forests, a unique combination of towering conifers, smaller moss-covered vine maples, swordlike ferns and soft ground cover. (Gene Ahrens Photo)

OLYMPIC NATIONAL PARK

At Olympic National Park, in Washington, the civilizaton of man defers almost totally to the civilization of the tree. Amid these thousands of acres of mountain and coastal wilderness, 50 miles wide and 200 miles in circumference, the tropical-like luxuriance of rain forests vies in beauty and splendor with the majestic eminence of an immense conifer empire on primeval coasts and on the flanks of soaring peaks.

Such is man's deferment to this almost preternatural infinitude of green — the hushed, eternal realm of the Sitka spruce, Western hemlock, Douglas fir and red cedar, among others — that park trail crews often cut narrow, wandering foot trails through the wilderness. In the forest depths abound the natural civilization of wildlife and wildflowers — the animals, birds, and both familiar and exotic blooms, which flourish in a protective privacy redolent of the legendary preserves of Adam and Eve.

The Strait of Juan de Fuca separates the park area from Canada. In 1774 the Spanish sea captain Juan Perez sailed through these waters of splendor, discovering the Olympic Mountains and originally calling them El Cerro de la Santa Rosalia. It remained for Capt. John Meares of Great Britain to explore the area in 1778 during which he named the highest peak "Mount Olympus," a designation later charted by Capt. George Vancouver.

Pacific Ocean tides break, ebb and flow against the park's western shoreline. Eastward, Puget Sound and Hood Canal form the added gift of isolation, separating, with saltwater barriers, the peninsula and mainland of Washington State.

Along the fascinating shores, isolated conifers, twisted and misshapen, dot the shorelines. Then the fragmented shore, the home of the seal and wildfowl life of the sea, yields to sheer cliffs, fog-shrouded or sparkling in the sun, depending upon the day's weather. This massive moisture-channeling, aided by 142 inches of annual rainfall, nourishes, on the western side, the finest remains of the Pacific Northwest rain forests.

The overwhelming impression of the rain forest is in Andrew Marvell's phrase: "a green lamp in a green shade." Or as one park service man said: "When one is inside the forest and the sun comes out, it is like being inside a giant emerald."

The lordly conifers dominate the realm, but here in the rain forest, the lesser fiefdoms of the tree kingdom are big-leaved and slender vine maples, burdened into arches by heavy veils of clubmoss. Most of this subsidiary civilization of the tree flourishes in openings under the dense conifer canopy.

The disappearance of the great rain forests, which once covered a coastal area from northern California to southern Alaska, highlights the preciousness of this magnificent "remnant" in Olympic National Park. It is almost as if a splendid tropical jungle lies at the foot of the more typically Northwestern snow-covered peaks which pierce the clouds at elevations of 3,000 to 8,000 feet. Majestic Mount Olympus dominates the uplands where more than sixty glaciers grow and recede, and these twenty-five square miles of ice hone down the mountains in the slow, eternal movement of time.

This mountainous interior lay unexplored until the winter of 1889-1890 when James H. Christie led the *Seattle Press* Expedition on the first crossing from Port Angeles to the Pacific Ocean. That summer Lt. Joseph P. O'Neil led another expedition, crossing the mountains from Hood Canal to the Pacific.

Lt. O'Neil was the first to propose that the mountains would "serve admirably for a national park." A first step occurred in 1897 when President Cleveland created the Olympic Forest Reserve. A portion of the reserve was set aside as Mount Olympus National Monument by that champion of outdoor life, President Theodore Roosevelt, in 1909. The long struggle for the permanent preservation of this vast retreat of nature ended in 1938, when Olympic National Park was established under another Roosevelt, F.D.R. Further land additions were made, expanding the park to its authorized expanse of nearly 1,400 square miles.

Mount Shuksan thrusts its 9,038-foot height above the autumn foliage at Picture Lake. (Bob and Ira Spring Photo)

NORTH CASCADES
NATIONAL PARK

Warm breath freezes in the wet coldness of the dark morning, as the mountains await the sun's heat. From the east, the first rays of the coming day edge over the vast land forms, and one by one the dawn's fingers touch the great peaks, illuminating their snow with a pink, then orange, and finally white light. The mists on the upper peaks begin to break and slowly dissipate, and the full majesty of these mountains comes into view.

To hike these valleys and climb the peaks is one of the most rewarding mountaineering adventures in North America. Montana's Glacier National Park and the Grand Tetons of Wyoming have their glories, but the vast rock cathedrals of Washington's northern Cascades have a scope and grandeur all their own.

Sometimes called the American Alps, these peaks, valleys and lakes sculpted by huge glaciers are considered by many outdoorsmen to be the most scenic mountain wilderness in the conterminous U.S.

The Cascade Range stretches from British Columbia to northern California, but the North Cascades in Washington contain more spectacular scenery than any other section.

The high mountains intercept some of the wettest prevailing Pacific Ocean winds. Their heavy precipitation has produced a region of hanging glaciers, ice-falls, ice caps, hanging valleys, waterfalls and alpine lakes nestled in glacial cirques. There are about 318 glaciers, most of which are stable or slightly retreating, and numerous snowfields within the North Cascades complex, which includes the north and south units of the park and Ross Lake and Lake Chelan national recreation areas — over a thousand square miles of mountain wilderness.

Over 130 alpine lakes dot the landscape and innumerable streams and creeks rush down the mountainsides, forming graceful waterfalls. Lake Chelan near Stehekin occupies a glacial trough exceeding 8,500 feet in depth, one of the deepest gorges on the continent. Fifty-five miles long and one to two miles wide, it has all the features of a Norwegian fjord.

Rain and an average of 516 inches of snow fall on the west side of the Cascades annually for a

A young mule deer stands at attention in the evergreen forests of the Cascades. (Ray Atkeson Photo)

total of 110 inches of precipitation. On the drier, eastern slopes, however, the precipitation averages only thirty-four inches. The Cascade Range is thus responsible for the semiarid plains of eastern Washington.

Naturally there is extreme variation in plant communities between the moisture-laden west side and the dry east slopes. From western rain forests, the vegetation changes to subalpine conifers, verdant meadows and alpine tundra, and then to eastern pine forests and sunny, dry shrublands. The valleys and mountains below the timberline are covered with dense stands of huge Douglas firs, tall hemlocks and Western red cedars, Engelmann and Sitka spruce, ponderosa

and lodgepole pines and silver firs. Mixed with the conifers are many deciduous trees — alders, maples, willows and cottonwoods, among others. In the wet valleys on the western slopes, moss grows so profusely that it hangs from the trees.

Supreme Court Justice William O. Douglas, who has hiked this region for a long lifetime, has written, "The wilderness of the North Cascades is a national resource of the future, not merely a local commodity, and we need it all, as a nation." This park of towering, craggy ice mountains, flashing streams and waterfalls, blue alpine lakes, forested valleys, colorful flowers and abundant widlife is, by any test, one of the crowning gems of the National Park System.

Moisture-laden clouds sweep over Mount Rainier which stands in the pale colors of dusk. (Victor Scheffer Photo)

MOUNT RAINIER NATIONAL PARK

Rainier stands like a silent sentinel over the Cascade Range, a color covering of blue and green and tones of gray, clad in the white cap of cold and age, a garment which belies its fiery parentage.

The mountain soars above the Cascade Mountains of west-central Washington, rising 14,410 feet above sea level, her size so ponderous she covers a quarter of the national park's almost 380 square miles.

Deep, green stands of trees, alpine lakes, the diamond-tipped rush of icy water crashing over smooth boulders, delicate flowers hidden in shady glens, sprawling wildflower meadows — all are subdued by the spectacle of ice, laced like a child's finger painting across the faces of Mount Rainier. It has the greatest expanse of glaciers — about forty in number — found in the United States outside of Alaska.

Rainier, part of that once-spectacular circle of volcanic activity which rings the Pacific from the Americas to Asia, was not always so placid, so gently touched or so green. Volcanic eruptions flowed lava upon lava, cinders upon ash, until the mountain grew with a fury nuclear energy cannot match. The Cascades to the east were created in the same manner, but Rainier retains more than a casual birthmark. At the summit are three peaks: Columbia Crest to the east, then two smaller but obvious volcanic craters. The summit crater on Columbia Crest retains small vents which whisper steam into the thin air.

Now Rainier is quiet. Time, water and glaciers have worn great canyons and raised ridges along its once-smooth sides, and glaciers now spread across its body, square mile after square mile of slowly flowing ice, an active reminder of the natural forces which helped shape much of our landscape today.

Clouds and fog often obscure the mountain. There is, however, usually warm, clear weather from about July 1 to mid-September. In many years, Indian summer weather continues well into October, when autumn colors bring out still another kind of quality possessed by this magnificent mountain and the land that surrounds it.

Overleaf: From Sunrise, the mountain looms skyward. (J. H. Burnett Photo)

MOUNT McKINLEY NATIONAL PARK

The Wilderness of Denali is not tamed. It is raw and primal, and a man feels very small in it. Almost anywhere off the one road he is truly alone — and sometimes a little afraid.

It is a vast land, which dwarfs normal scales. Sprawling river bars, peopled with the swarming specks that are the caribou, wind out of immensity at the foot of the hills. The wind across the tundra is clean, untainted by mankind.

The spirit of the wolf hangs over the land. Unseen, his presence is felt. He is the warden and unwitting benefactor of the caribou, the superb culmination of the biotic pyramid — and the personification of the wild.

Over all, the Alaska Range rises in a succession of brilliant ridges and cornices — each magnificent in its own right, but nearly lost in the greater picture. Higher they rise, leading the eye to the massive upsurge that is *The Mountain*. A full three vertical miles above the living tundra soars its peak.

Nothing lives on the mountain, but the mountain lives. Avalanches leap from its walls. Seracs crash; glaciers rumble and grind. Clouds swirl about its flanks, and a snow plume is torn by the wind from its uppermost crests. In the evening, the glare of the eternal ice softens, glows with the color of fireweed, then pales to ivory against the darkened sky.

It is fortunate that one of the earliest explorers of the area was a naturalist and conservationist. Charles Sheldon, hunting specimens for the National Museum, roamed the country for three years and felt its impact. Recognizing the intrinsic value of the landscape and its wildlife, he conceived the idea of making the area a national park while camping there in the summer of 1906. His vigorous efforts to create a refuge for the swarming wildlife, aided by the Boone and Crockett Club, brought about the establishment of Mount McKinley National Park just eleven years later. Today it is the only park service area which harbors the white Dall sheep and the barren grounds caribou, and its 3,030 square miles embrace more untouched wilderness than any other national park.

Mountaineers answered the challenge of Mount McKinley early. On April 6, 1910, a hardy group of sourdoughs climed to the summit of the north peak of McKinley, carrying with them a fourteen-foot spruce pole. It was an astonishing feat, for the group was inexperienced and poorly equipped. Modern mountaineers find the climb as dangerous and demanding as a Himalayan expedition, but each year a few manage to stand atop the continent.

Relatively little has changed since Sheldon fought to make this area a park. A single graveled road winds its leisurely way eighty-six miles into the park, climbing from the deep green spruce of the taiga to the sweeping tapestry of the alpine tundra. You may see from the road the same wild peaks and teeming wildlife that thrilled the first visitors. Over the tundra range groups of caribou, the bulls in late summer bearing brilliant white capes and towering, blood-red antlers. Moose, looking shiny black at a little distance, feed knee-deep in ponds or browse in willow thickets.

The deceptively lethargic-looking grizzly keeps his head down, gobbling berries, roots and grasses. Red foxes trot across the road, seemingly indifferent to man. Ptarmigan erupt into the air with a humorous, guttural croaking, their white wings flashing in startling contrast to their barred brown bodies.

In the ponds everywhere beavers are busy cutting willow. Golden eagles soar above. Gyrfalcons are sometimes seen, and marsh hawks swoop low across the dry flats. On the lower peaks, a spray of white dots becomes a flock of Dall sheep.

If you are very lucky, you may see a wolf. When you have seen the eyes of the wolf, you have seen the quintessence of wildness.

Opposite: Wonder Lake and Mount McKinley are captured at summer sunset. (FPG Photo)

KATMAI NATIONAL MONUMENT

Welcome to The Last Wilderness. Although other states may have patches of wilderness, only Alaska's is so primeval and untamed that you could wander for weeks without seeing another human being. It is the kind of wilderness that even people who know they will never see it are deeply satisfied that it still exists. Katmai National Monument, one of the largest units of the National Park System, protects over 4,200 square miles of this wilderness.

Located on the east coast of the peninsula leading to the Aleutian chain, this is one of the least visited in the U.S. parks. The annual visitor rate can be counted in the hundreds; in Yosemite National Park that many people may visit every hour. And it is this very lack of human intrusion that keep Katmai wild and beautiful. With no road or rail access, the monument is out of reach for the casual tourist. Private or chartered planes are needed to see the most scenic spots, for scheduled flights from the King Salmon airport on the Bering Sea side of the peninsula go only to Brooks River lodge and campground. Such isolation guarantees protection of prime wilderness values.

Katmai contains three distinct geographic sections. To the east is the seacoast on Shelikof Strait, a coastline of unsurpassed beauty. The central part is a series of deep fjords nearly surrounded by cliffs rising abruptly one thousand or more feet above the blue waters. The northern and southern coasts are comprised of wide, shallow bays with many extensive sandy beaches bordering large marshes and, in Katmai Valley to the south, treacherous quicksand. Offshore are many small islets where Pacific hair seals and northern sea lions rest from the often turbulent waters of the strait. The great gray whale sometimes hunts in the bays and the northern sea otter plays in the shallows.

Inland from the coast is the Aleutian Mountain Range, forming the backbone of Katmai. These snow-capped peaks, as high as 7,600 feet, are continually being carved by glaciers and some of them are active volcanoes. There is little vegetation here because of the cold, the high winds and the short growing season; what does exist is of the subarctic tundra variety.

In the western portion of the monument is a huge mixture of grasslands, green forests and large, deep blue lakes. Two life zones meet here as on the seacoast: the Arctic zone above two thousand feet, comprised of short grasses and other low-lying vegetation; and the Hudsonian zone of forests of white spruce, balsam poplar, paper birch and dense stands of reed grass. Gradually the woodlands are replacing the grasslands in this part of the monument; the increased rainfall and milder climate of recent years has induced a rapid growth of trees.

Large mammals are numerous. The largest of them, the Alaskan brown bear, can be seen during summer in and along the streams as it fishes for salmon coming up the waters to spawn. In other seasons the bears eat grass on the open slopes, dig for roots or gorge themselves on the wild berries that are abundant in autumn. Moose are common and will always be found near the waters of the

One in a chain of active volcanoes, Martin Volcano lies south of the Valley of Ten Thousand Smokes. (Shelly Grossman Photo)

lakes or larger streams. Wolverines, the most far-ranging small mammals — found from sea level to three thousand feet — snarl at visitors if their prey is frightened away by man's approach. River otters are numerous on the lakes and along the shores of the bays.

The most abundant meat-eater at Katmai is the red fox, normally found in the lower elevations of the western portions of the monument. The lynx is the only member of the cat family living in this region and sometimes can be seen in the monument headquarters area at Brooks River.

Beavers "log" the woods near the lakes and build large dams. Caribou and reindeer were once plentiful but have decreased to the point where none have been seen for many years.

Perhaps the most interesting mammal at Katmai is the wolf. This animal's howl is the trademark of the true wilderness. No other species has been so misunderstood by man. We now know that the vicious, man-eating wolf is a myth. Although in rare instances wolves have attacked man, they are wary of him and normally shun all areas where man intrudes.

HALEAKALA NATIONAL PARK

The land sleeps here now, resting under the warm Pacific sun after the long day geologists count in millions of years. To Haleakala (pronounced HA-lay-ah-kah-LA), it is night and a well-deserved rest, for this Hawaiian volcano helped form the lovely green fingers that probe the sea as part of our fiftieth state.

To Polynesians, it means "House of the Sun," and it was once that, belching forth angry torrents of fire and lava, making night as day, until it subsided in placid surrender to time, leaving as a heritage one of the showplaces of the National Park System so that all might understand the forces of geological evolution.

On a clear day — and there are many in the Pacific — the summit affords a spectacular view of the neighboring islands of Hawaii, Lanai, Molokai and occasionally Oahu. Turn the eyes a bit downward, and unfolding beyond the crater's rim is a vast hole in the earth, gouged by water erosion, leaving acres of symmetrical cinder cones painted with primeval colors huddled inside great formations of cliffs whose tops are hidden in the moist clouds, lending even more vastness to the gigantic, dormant crater seven and a half miles long and two and a half miles wide.

The House of the Sun is quiet now, for no eruptions have occurred here for centuries. But there is the appeal of something new, raw, a just-formed land, and in geological terms it is that. Lava is sterile stuff, for nothing can survive its heat. Generations of plant life have rained down upon the cool rock until, in places, anyway, here and there a plant has been able to gain a foothold. That is fortunate, for they will flourish, then die, deepening the topsoil by a fraction of a millimeter so that other plants might follow eventually.

Life grows slowly at Haleakala National Park, for this is still a new land. But the silversword has fought grazing animals, man and the barren beds of lava to thrust its spheres of silvery, dagger-shaped leaves and three to seven-foot flowers, casting to the four winds thousands of seeds, then dying — the first handful of compost to fertilize the silent mountain.

When viewed from the rim above Kapalaoa Cabin, hikers can see the nineteen-square-mile crater floor many feet below the summit. (R. Wenkam Photo)

HAWAII VOLCANOES NATIONAL PARK

Huge mountains, their gray, lifeless sides warmed by the Pacific sun, spout their anger at the placid blue seas around them, belching fountains of lava and red fire into the sky, pouring orange-red streams of molten rock down unresisting slopes.

This is a link with the past — geological history in the making as the Hawaiian Islands continue to emerge from the sea as they first did five to ten million years ago. Hawaii Island, largest of the chain, is the site of Mauna Loa, a 13,680-foot summit where Hawaii Volcanoes National Park begins, stretching southeast to the seacoast, a place of contrasts where umbrella-shaped palms and dense jungles of ferns lie near gaunt mountains and beside lava deserts.

The region has fascinated visitors for more than a century. The Rev. William Ellis, a British missionary, saw it in 1823 and said in his *A Tour Through Hawaii*: "... A spectacle, sublime and even appalling, presented itself before us. We stopped and trembled. Astonishment and awe for some moments rendered us mute.... The bottom was covered with lava, and the southwest and northern parts of it were one vast flood of burning matter, in a stage of terrific ebullition, rolling to and fro its 'fiery surge' and flaming billows."

The spectacle of the volcano, Kilauea, impressed Mr. Ellis and countless thousands since. Within the volcano at that time, at Halemaumau, was a great lake of rolling lava which spread across the floor, and at other times seeped into earth fissures to produce avalanches of fire. A later visitor stared at the sight, then told a guide, "I've seen hell. Now I want to go home." This "lava-lake" phase ceased with the steam explosion of 1924.

From the eleven-mile Crater Rim Drive around the summit caldera of Kilauea volcano, Kilauea Crater, the visitor can see the destruction wrought by the forces of nature — cones of cinder, bluffs alive with steam and recent flows of lava. One of the most impressive sections is the "devastated area," which was denuded of vegetation during the 1959 eruptions of Kilauea Iki. The ancient Hawaiians made a deity of Pele, the goddess of volcanoes, whom they believed lived in Halemaumau, Kilauea's most active vent. It was her wrath, they said, which caused the eruptions, destroying villages and tilled lands.

From the summit caldera, the visitor passes along the Chain of Craters, part of the east rift of the volcano where the road winds past deep craters in which eruptions have recently taken place. In March 1965, a fissure on the side of Makaopuhi Crater poured forth a lake of lava almost three hundred feet deep. During the 1959 eruption of Kilauea Iki, lava spewed more than 1,900 feet high, filling a crater with molten lava to a depth of about four hundred feet. Until recently, the most spectacular of all volcanoes here was Mauna Loa, but it has not erupted since 1950.

From Makaopuhi Crater near the end of the chain, the island's newest scenic road passes along the southeast coast, past ancient villages and sites of religious temples. The mighty mountains of fire must have prompted these peoples to great religious fervor. At Wahaula Heiau near the eastern edge of the park is one of the island's best-known places of worship where it is reputed that one of the last human sacrifices was performed under the old religion.

Now the religion is appreciation of and humility before nature, which is protected within the boundaries of this park in a subtropical corner of paradise.

Overleaf: Effervescing several hundred feet, the lava fountain is considered to be relatively gentle. (National Park Service Photo)